Grow Thin

While You Sleep!

Grow Thin While You Sleep!

Daya Devi-Doolin

Padaran Publications

Deltona, FL 32725

Grow Thin While You Sleep! Copyright © 2014, Daya Devi-Doolin, Padaran Publications, Deltona, FL 32725.

All Rights Reserved, including the right to reproduce the book, or any portion thereof, in any form without prior permission of the Publisher, except for the inclusion of brief quotations in a review. Excerpts from *Super Vita-Minds: How to Stop Saying I Hate You...To Yourself*, Padaran Publications, Deltona, FL 32725. The First Edition of A Course in Miracles is now free from copyright. We are quoting from the First Edition.

Publisher's Note

The Publisher and Author shall have neither liability nor responsibility to any person or organization with respect to any loss or damage caused or alleged to be caused directly or indirectly by the information contained in this book. The purpose of this book is to educate, entertain and stimulate. This book is sold with the understanding that the Publisher and Author are not involved in offering legal, medical or psychological services. If any assistance is required, the services of a competent professional should be sought. In addition, it is not the purpose of this book to be used in the diagnosis of any medical or psychological condition.

ISBN   978 1877945 20 5
        First Edition   1 2 3 4 5 6 7 8 9 10
Sales: (386) 532-5308
Email: padaran@padaran.com
Graphic Designer & Photographers Dario Shields
Back Cover Bob Dominguez
www.darioashields.com
Model: Ashley Donaldson

Printed in the United States of America
Padaran Publications
1794 N. Acadian Dr.
Deltona, FL 32725

Books Written by Daya Devi-Doolin

Grow Thin While You Sleep!
The Only Way Out Is In: The Secrets of the 14 Realms to Love, Happiness and Success!
Super Vita-Minds: How To Stop Saying I Hate You…To Yourself
Americans Saving Ourselves Together: How to Thrive in the 21st Century
Dabney's Handbook on A Course in Miracles
All I Need to Know….Is Inside (A Pocket Bite Book with cartoons)
Dabney, Dormck & Wiggles' Slakaduman Adventures
Dormck and the Temple of the Healing Light
Sikado's Star of Aragon (Dabney & Dormck Adventures)

Books Written by Chris & Daya Devi-Doolin

Hidden Manna: How You Too Can Interpret Your Dreams
Returning to The Source
Smile America

Attention healing transformational centers, schools of spiritual growth, and organizations: quantity discounts are available on bulk purchases of Daya Devi-Doolin's books for educational purposes or fund raising. For information, please contact Padaran Publications, 1794 N. Acadian Drive, Deltona, FL 32725; www.padaran.com or call. We thank you for your support and bless you in your growth.

Table of Contents

Acknowledgement		i
Foreword		iii
Introduction		vii
1	Creative Mind - The Master of Your Success	1
2	Do you Figure it Doesn't Matter?	7
3	How to Recognize Your Stumbling Blocks	11
4	Feeling, Imagining, Believing	21
5	Building a Consciousness of Thinness	25
6	How to BE Thin Right Now	29
7	Grow Thin While You Sleep	37
8	What Are You Willing to Change?	41
9	Grow Thin While Helping Others	49
10	You Are Thin Right Now	55
Summary		59
Appendix		63
About the Author		71
The Anointed & Appointed Ones		73

Acknowledgment

"Trust in the Lord with all your heart, and lean not on your own understanding; in all your ways acknowledge Him and He shall direct your paths." Proverbs 3: 5-6

I am acknowledging all the love and support I have received from my father and mother, Leon and Sallie Brown, who are in another dimension and who raised me to know the Peace of God by their own Being-ness and to Chris my dear husband of 38 years. He never lets me forget how glad he is that I am from another dimension, and how much he loves me and my sons Tyler and Joseph. My two sons always tell and show me how glad they are that the Lord made me and how beautiful I am. My youngest son Joseph just told me the other day "You are an Angel!"

Specifically, I thank my dear husband, Chris, for supporting me in every unimaginable way. I could not have done what I have done without you, your ideas, your forever love and support. You are the most nurturing, caring, funny and BEST friend in every way to me. Love you!

I am grateful to my Ascended Master Brothers and Sisters, specifically the Christ, Ezekiel, St. Germain and Kwan Yin who are the Holy Beings who have been my constant Guides. I am deeply grateful to have been touched in this way by their love and guidance.

In honor of all those appointed and anointed ones I am gifted to call my friends and family who helped me heal, they are Dr. Leon Brown (my deceased brother), my sisters Dirdrah Watson, Dara Brown and my nieces, Michael Brown my brother, Debbie Moran, Felicia Benzo, Pete Esquinaldo, Dan Towey, Bill and Gail Crippen, Bob and Iris Reynolds, Bob and Maria Dominguez, Drs. Phil and Nalani

Valentine, Inez Bracy, Zo Clement, Healers International, Diane Fisher, Victoria Moran, Patti Collins, Mari Leisen and Lisa Ghofrani.

I want to thank everyone who purchases and reads this book, for desiring to know the Truth, to practice the principles within, and to live the Truth to the best of their Being-ness.

Glory Be to God!

Foreword

People like Judge Howard Troward, Charles and Myrtle Fillmore, Jose´ Silva, Neville Goddard, Dr. Helen Schumann, Dr. William Thetford, Deepak Chopra, Dr. Wayne Dyer, Catherine Ponder, Dr. Ernest Holmes, Dr. Emmet Fox, Genevieve Behrend, Florence Scovel Shinn and others like them regard the importance of holding the power of thought in the highest regard. I have read and studied Neville's books, audios and lectures, Godfrey Ray King's, *Magic I am Presence*, Charles and Myrtle Fillmore, and others and they have all taught me the importance of our intention, thought, imagination, believing and the power they hold to change our world first – our inner world. Then we can see the changes take place in our outer world for a better world to materialize or the world that was hidden from our vision because we had a different consciousness about things around us.

Apparently, long before I realized it, I was chosen to join their ranks in helping to make others strong so they too can be healthy in mind, body, spirit and affairs, free to live without fear. Helping people to learn how to heal physically, emotionally, mentally and spiritually saves them unnecessary doctor bills, the ill side effects of the drugs sometimes offered to them haphazardly. I have learned through Spirit's guidance to use my mind because it has the Power to heal myself, my family and others.

It is my intention to continue to support and to promote and offer healing, to meet, to offer workshops, to facilitate classes on holistic and spiritual healing, to promote and gain greater acceptance and recognition for the use of spiritual healing and to provide a forum for the exchange of information to further holistic and spiritual ideals for the health and spiritual growth of our community and the world.

It has been my intention and I have done so in the past, to assist those parents who have children who have been abused or molested. They were referred to me and to use our natural healing facility. I was a Non-Clinical Professional with the corporation called *ACT* in that manner. I understand the great joy of being in service for the purpose of releasing fear from the World and bringing in a world of Peace and Love.

The Center, my husband Chris and I co-founded years ago, *The Doolin Healing Sanctuary,* is a metaphysical learning and healing center which offers programs and classes and services aimed at total, complete and permanent healing of the Whole self and on integrating the Whole self into the I AM.

Healing enhances a more centered life-style, more spiritual clarity and a healthier disposition, and enhances attitudinal and cellular changes. My intention has been to reach out globally and continue to "Make a Difference in the World."

"When you say "I AM" you assert the reality of your existence-not the mere reality of the physical existence, which is but temporary and relative-but your real existence in the Spirit, which is not temporary or relative, but is eternal and absolute. The real "I" is not body, but is the Spirit principle which is manifesting in body and mind."
~Yogi Ramacharaka

Introduction

On October 25, 2011, a young male motorist in his twenties crossed over three lanes of traffic while texting and within seconds had plowed into my car as I sat parked at a stop sign waiting to emerge onto 17-92 Highway. I was with my oldest son, Tyler and our pet dog Pookey. We had just come from having the Vet check out her ear which had a hematoma.

I was told ambulance workers had to cut the car apart to pull me out and I was airlifted by helicopter for emergency surgery. My oldest son Ty called my husband Chris who was at work. I was unconscious for several hours.

Unbeknownst to me, Chris took photos which showed my car was put into reverse, though I don't recall doing it. I later found out why it was put in reverse as I will soon explain.

Before the accident, my weight was between 172 - 175 lbs. By 2012, I had gone up to 189 pounds. During that time of healing, I had to eat whatever my family was able to make for me and what friends were able to prepare for us. I had to make up my mind that I could do something to reverse what was taking place. This book is the result of the change, that intention, that desire with the guidance of Spirit.

My healing had improved enough, so I resumed teaching Hatha Yoga to my students. I was not able to move into my postures as I used to because of burning, stiffness and swelling of my left shoulder and arm. It was a little disheartening to say the least having been practicing and teaching for fifty-plus years. I could walk, but not for very long like I used to, so exercising was done in my mind like athletes do to gear up for a game, tennis, etc. My energy was not back to normal.

My brother, Dr. Leon A. Brown (I called him Lee) passed away two weeks before my accident and he died in Cleveland, Ohio. As I would normally go out in my front yard and sit on our park bench under the front trees to meditate, I did the same this particular day of my healing. Sitting there quietly, my brother, Lee's spirit came to me. He said, "Do you know why you put your car in reverse when you were supposed to have your foot on the brake while waiting to emerge? I told you to put the car in reverse and you did as I told you. You would have been killed if you hadn't followed my instructions. By your putting the car in reverse, it saved your life. I am with you." We spoke more after that but not much and when we were done, two Cardinals flew down and sat to my left on the grass about 3-4 feet away. They were husband and wife and it seemed as if they were saying, "And So It Is – Amen. Yes you did actually hear from him." I started tearing and giving thanks to God and to him.

Though the motorist called the hospital to see how I was, if I was dead or going to make it, he legally was not supposed to do that I was told by the lawyers. He spoke with my husband Chris and told him he was glad to hear I was going to make it. I've never heard from him since. I forgave him for creating such a horrendous experience. I had to have two surgeries; one to heal a broken left humerus bone and the other to heal the AC joint (which joins the clavicle and shoulder joint). I had never had surgery before in my life to deal with, except to have tonsils removed as a child and one to correct crossed eyes at 2 yrs. old. The stitches were done with staples and healing tape which was absolutely excruciating to bear. But Chris bore it with me, tenderly taking care of me.

I had to get up to go to the bathroom 3-4 times a night for many weeks and I needed his help through that. At the same time, he had to get up at 6 am for getting ready for work. I did not like having to disturb his sleep but he said just nudge him. When I nudged him, he never said "Oh no". He only said, "You ready to rock and roll?" and he'd hop up right away. Not wanting to wake him after a few weeks of this, I figured out how to grab hold of the bed sheets with my right hand and pull myself up with much difficulty and get up to sit on the edge of the bed. Then I did not wake him so early, only to get me to walk to the bathroom. Soon we rigged up a chair in the shower, so I could lower myself down onto the seat and pull myself up by the chair rung without the chair falling or slipping over.

I moved from him having to personally care for me, to doing it myself. I was proud of myself at being able to do this tiny feat.

Coming home from the hospital after the first surgery to repair a broken humerus bone in my left upper arm, I had to return a week later to repair the AC joint because the clavicle was sticking up through my shoulder covered by skin.

Chris waited until I was dismissed from hospital on good behavior (healing quickly). As I said earlier, I never had surgery before. No one told me what to expect going in or coming out or the aftermath to expect. I had to wear a sling and keep my arm still twenty-four hours a day– sleeping and waking. No bra.

Going to the bathroom every 2-3 hrs, waking my husband Chris, his comment each time, "You ready to rock 'n roll?" would make me laugh despite the pain I was going through to get up. He was pretty cheerful about it despite having to wake up for work every morning and get our youngest son up for high school.

He would come to my side of the bed, reach out his right arm and hand to assist me getting up. I really did not look forward to having to wake him up during the night. I felt guilty but there was no other way. He'd stand in front of me and wait until I was ready to grip his helping hand.

I would sleep in one spot for twelve hours with the exception of getting up for restroom break with my left arm raised in the sling and up on a rolled pillow to my left. My arm was swollen, my guitar fingers swollen three times normal size. My mind (my ego self) tried to scare me for several weeks until I decided I didn't like scaring myself. I gave my healing over to God, my Christ consciousness for peace of mind and seeing the end result for my goals to be realized.

I had to have goals for myself each day no matter how small or insignificant others might have thought they were. My oldest son Ty was there every day to help me too with small tasks, to make breakfast, lunch and snacks for me when my youngest son Joseph and Chris were not there.

I made a goal to listen to what I heard from Spirit for that day, that week. This time I made the intention to take myself to the bathroom by grabbing hold of the flannel bed sheet with my right hand, arm in the sling and with several tries, I could swing my legs to left side of the bed and pull myself up with the sheet. This way I didn't have to disturb Chris. When he found out what I had done, he was so stunned and surprised and grateful I had accomplished this on my own. He had rigged a chair to be halfway in the shower stall and over the rim of the shower stall onto the floor so I could lower myself and raise myself without trouble and the chair would not slip. It was so hard getting down and up but my goal was to get better and better and to *believe* I was getting better and better each and every day 100%.

I was getting used to Chris washing me, washing my hair in the shower and dressing me. I couldn't wash under my arms or shampoo my hair myself. I could brush my teeth alone but tons of things I could no longer do because of immobility, pain of the tape, stitches and the auto accident aftermath.

On getting dressed, it was very painful to move my arm, no bra was possible and I had worn one since I was thirteen years old, or so it felt very strange for me. Chris took me to department stores to buy a strapless bra or two. With assistance from my husband and youngest son I was able to wear it. We had to look for weeks to find the perfect strapless bras in my size. Still Chris was mostly the one to adjust it in the back. Other bras irritated the stitches and the new scar along my shoulder so I had a few months to go before the bra reality could come about.

January 15, 2012, on the Dr. Martin Luther King Jr. Holiday, we decided to look in the papers for car dealers. But first we took a piece of paper and drew a line down the middle. Chris wrote down what he wanted in a car. I wrote down what I wanted. Then we decided to check out some car dealers. We went to one car dealer, our first one and found out the first car we saw was what we liked. We bought it right away. No thinking or wondering about it. This all came about because of imagining beforehand, feeling it real, feeling it complete, believing and following intuition or the guidance given us by Creative Mind. I'll delve more into this in later chapters.

We knew after our plans – this was the car that wanted to come home with us. It is an Audi A3 and we wanted a safe car, luxurious one and it had to be the right shade, a metallic blue. I didn't drive it until January 24 or 25th. It was my first time driving since that October 25th day of the accident.

That was when I started driving myself to the rehabilitation office twice a week in the afternoons. Up until January 26th, Joseph had been the one driving me to my occupational therapy sessions.

I had to push fears aside and call on my faith, courage, Christ Mind and belief that I could drive again and be safe from harm.

In my mind, I wanted to play my guitar again. In my mind, it was no problem. Getting my mind and fingers coordinated was not working but Chris kept affirming it would happen and not to worry. I arranged with him to set up gig dates that would motivate me to get myself ready at least to play one song on the guitar. It worked. We performed Dec. 23rd together. I played "My Declaration" the musical score performed during credits of the movie, "Ink Heart". I had my sling on under my beautiful silver Jennifer Lopez blouse and a grey Jennifer Lopez jazzy leggings with puffy Jopher type pockets. I sang on the rest of our set with Chris. I sat on a stool. I was worn out after the first set and didn't sing during the other sets. I gave myself applauses for accomplishing our goals. Each week I'd set up in my mind pictures (images) of where I'd be practicing my chords. Sometimes because of the swelling of my fingers it hurt to try to curl them around the strings and or press them down. I never gave up the belief that I would eventually be able to do so. On January 30, 2012, I heard to take out my songbook and try again. This time instead of one song and getting frustrated, I went through four songs – still a little frustrated when I could not play a C chord or remember how to finger it, I did it. This was HUGE!! We performed that coming Friday and the first Friday of each month. I told myself, Creative Mind that I'll be able to perform at least four songs very well by then. I was thrilled with myself. Singing was no problem. Fingering and pressing down the strings was still a challenge. But when you love something, you think of yourself as practicing for the Olympics like other Olympian wannabes and you keep on regardless of the frustration, the flubs, and the mistakes until you accomplish what you see in your mind that is shown to you to do and that you can do. Creative Mind kept me doing everything I believed I could do and kept manifesting the gigs for us so I could prove to myself I could do it. I finally mastered four chords – played 4 songs very roughly, but I did it.

You already know you must keep your body flexible, moving and eating right so I won't dwell on what I think is the best exercise program for you. Personally, yoga is my purpose and has been for fifty plus years.

In my regimen, I needed to get lots of veggies and fruit in my food intake and I chose to use the Nutribullet (www.nutribullet.com) to extract my vitamins and minerals. I did so for increasing my health, keeping my cells bathed in optimum natural nutrients and organic where and when possible.

So now, do you want to transform your life today? Do you want to have your own business; do you want to be slimmer, healthier, wealthier, and happier;so to sp do you want a better relationship or a healed one, a new home? You can use the universal principles I explain here for any solution of any problem. You can become the president of your own company, and you can be in a beautiful loving relationship and you are right this minute in your state of Imagination if you don't give up and keep persisting.

Why don't we start heading towards *Grow Thin While You Sleep* and I will gladly lead you to how the Law of Be-ing has worked in my life and how you can have IT work for you as well on any level of business, career, health, healing, releasing weight or improved relationships, guaranteed.

Thanks for taking me along with you on your journey. Enjoy the miracles that you are NOW ready to receive! Realize that the miracles are not one sided but are many faceted for all parts of your life. Do not be obsessed about your body. Love it as you grow into loving it more. Release your attack mode and allow; release and let God.

Chapter 1
Creative Mind - The Master of Your Success!

"The invisible forces are ever working for man who is always 'pulling the strings' himself, though he does not know it. Owing to the vibratory power of words, whatever man voices, he begins to attract."
~ *The Game of Life*, Florence Scovel Shinn

Creative Mind- The Master of Your Success!
    The power of thought is our inherited natural gift and the Universe is always in Total Agreement with whatever thoughts we hold true and entertain as truth. When you decide to live in the NOW and experience everything around you to the fullest, with love, you will see miracles become unhidden and become visible. There are Universal Principles such as Law of Mind, the Law of Cause and Effect and others like the Law of Attraction that are constant and unchanging waiting for us to call upon them with awareness.
    We are given the power and knowledge to work with them and utilize them as we align with them. Consciousness is IT! It creates the world we see and we are the directors of this VAST creation as God is always in Agreement with all our creations! We can change the script at any time we are ready to move on. As you move through your day, know the Holy Spirit is your Only Invited Guest. That is something I encourage you to fully realize, remember and utilize for any of your desires!
    Subconscious mind is another name used for creative mind. Other names for the same force are Infinite

Intelligence, Infinite Mind, and God-Mind, so if I use any of these terms, you'll know what I mean.

What Does Ego Do?

Ego's use of guilt, anger, blame, judgment or criticism keeps us in a prison and what we give out we receive while in that prison. What else does it do? It lives in fear, acts out of fear and blossoms into illusions glorified.

Giving is having and giving is receiving. If we give out judgmental thoughts, critical thought, words or deeds, it is exactly what we are proclaiming to manifest in our lives. That is what we will be receiving. You cannot give what you do not have. You cannot give love if you are un-loving; therefore you will not receive it or know that you have truly received it from the Universe on a parallel reality. What you give out comes back to you magnified.

We block the channel of good from coming to us because of our disbelief that it could happen. We would be able to see the miracle before our eyes if we were willing to change our perception about what we think we see. Changing our perception of what we see shows us the miracles that are before us.

We could ask the Holy Spirit to reveal the true meaning to us of what we see or experience. Instead of seeing ourselves as limited (ego's view of ourselves) and lacking, unhealthy, getting old, weary and unloved, we could turn those thoughts over to the Holy Spirit and begin to see ourselves as totally whole, safe and secure.

The vibration of these words alone such as, "I am whole, safe and protected", will make it so for you. "I am my perfect weight," will make it so too, for example. Saying, "I have more than enough money to have fun, travel and serve others," will heal you immediately. The Light from these words focuses energy into the dark cells of our being and irradiates love everywhere, within and without. It allows us to walk on water (turmoil in your life), as did Jesus Christ.

The next and important thing of life is to be totally GRATEFUL for everything you see around you happening, in your life and without. That is how we change things, by being grateful, not by being critical or judgmental of anything or anyone. Once you are grateful for the space in your consciousness that you have graduated to, you can move into an even more un-limiting consciousness and become more of a servant to mankind on an unconditional level. Being grateful de-crystallizes all negative energy blocks on a cellular, emotional/mental and spiritual level throughout the entire body.

When we put ego in its rightful place, which is that of a teacher instead of our Creator, we will automatically get off the treadmill of "I hate myself, I hate my life, I hate the world" consciousness. We can say, "Thank you, ego, for letting me know I do not want to be in this space anymore. Thank you for showing me there must be something better for me than this mentally, emotionally, physically debilitating space that I have mis-created. I am grateful that I can change. I am grateful I am Master of my Life!"

There is power in knowing we all have behind our intentions and thoughts the strength and courage to be the master of our lives. We have learned how thoughts are things and how to use them to our advantage. It is very important to change our perception about ourselves in order to see the miracles that are before us in a parallel reality.

Examples have been given on applying the principles and techniques in this chapter and will continue in each chapter. You can become empowered enough to know you can change your life, relationships, any illness or your weight, simply by the positive way you feel about yourself and by believing that you can do so through your imagination working with creative mind.

Anyone can come to realize she is a beautiful, loving being. We deserve all the love that is meant for us to have.

By faith in a Higher Power and the energy we put behind our faith, we can give our goals the power to manifest boldly and securely in our lives. What is there that is difficult to manifest in our lives? Nothing, if we but believe that it is possible.

Exercise:
Write it down now - What is it I want?
Write it down now - Why do I want it?
Write it down now – Why can't I have it?
Write it down now – Why do I think I can?

You'll get a lot of insight into yourself when you do this exercise.

Allow yourself to write down 100 or more answers for each question. The Creative Source of our Being is unlimited so don't limit yourself in what you can ask for or have.

One of my Nutribullet Recipes for increasing my health is below. Please understand, I am not a certified nutritionist or allopathic physician. I am, as I stated on the inside front cover, presenting this information for education and entertainment purposes.

Suggested Recipe with Nutribullet extractor
1/2 c washed spinach
5-6 frozen strawberries
3-4 chunks of frozen papaya
3-4 chunks of frozen mangoes
Add water to the MAX line and not more than that.
(Sometimes I add orange juice or lemon juice)
I screw the Nutribullet top on, turn on for 60 sec.
Unscrew the top and drink, ummmmm.

Brief Points of Chapter
- The power of thought is our inherited natural gift and God is always in Total Agreement with whatever thoughts we hold true and entertain as truth.
- We are given the power and knowledge to work with them and utilize them as we align with them. Consciousness is IT! It creates the world we see and we are the directors of this VAST creation as God is always in Agreement with all our creations!
- Ego's use of guilt, anger, blame, judgment or criticism keeps us in a prison and what we give out we receive while in that prison.
- Changing our perception of what we see shows us the miracles that are before us.
- You can become empowered enough to know you can change your life, relationships, any illness or your weight, simply by the positive way you feel about yourself and by believing that you can do so through your imagination working with creative mind.

Grow Thin While You Sleep!

Chapter 2
Do You Figure it Doesn't Matter?

"Keep thy heart (or imagination) with all diligence, for out of it are the issues of life." (Prov. 4:23.)

Do You Figure it Doesn't Matter?

"Whatsoever a man sows that shall he also reap." This means that whatever man sends out in word or deed, it will return to him; what he gives, he will receive.

It means that whatever man or woman images (thinks), sooner or later it becomes externalized in all his affairs. Ask yourself, "Do I think it doesn't matter what I think about? Do I figure I can think any thought and I will not see it represented in my external affairs?"

How do you feel about your decision to eat anything and think it will not matter since you are already overweight or obese? Having eaten one box of Oreo cookies, will it matter if you ate another box of Oreos or one more slice of pizza or one more piece of fried chicken?

Do you say, "What's the use in listening to that inner voice (which is the loving voice of the Holy Spirit) telling me I am already full, I don't need any more or I don't need to clean my plate?" If I say, 'I need to eat it now so it won't be around later to tempt me,' does it matter?"

We can decide now and that's what I am anticipating you are doing now, deciding to change your blueprint or pattern of thinking, to one where you realize that everything you think does matter if you wish to change your external world to one of success instead of failure. Many people reference Albert Einstein's saying about what insanity is. I'll use it here, "Insanity is doing the same thing over and over again and expecting different results." Using the same thought patterns, choosing to eat in the same way and the same foods which haven't worked for you is not benefitting you.

What is Imagination?

We must train our imaging faculty, our *creative mind* and give it new instructions and new directions. You are a person with an imaging faculty and you have the ability to train yourself (your *creative mind*) to imagine only good and bring good into your life, health, wealth, love, friends, perfect self-expression and your highest ideals.

Our imagination has been called, "The Gateway", and it is ever working on our behalf, in a good way or in a negative way. Sooner or later we meet our own creations in our external world based on the depth of our feeling and belief about the outcome. The Greeks have said: "Know Thyself."

We have a conscious mind which is concerned with seeing life as we think it appears. It sees death, sickness, poverty and limitation, etc. of every kind and it impresses the subconscious mind with its belief that what we see is true and is the truth. The subconscious mind is simply power, without direction. It does what it is directed to do with no judgment, only by the faith we have invested into it.

Whatever man feels deeply or images clearly is impressed upon the subconscious mind and carried out in the minutest detail. Our super conscious mind, our Higher Self is the God Mind within each man, and is the realm of perfection.

Imagination is our Immortal self. It precedes the desire fulfilled if the desire is not cancelled out by our disbelief. It creates our reality. If there is conflict between your conscious mind and your subconscious mind, what you image or imagine is delayed because of doubt and disbelief that it can be manifested. The subconscious mind will work on what you have the most faith in, the most belief in.

In our imagination, we want to be other than what we have created for ourselves. We have to be specific and begin to BE or appropriate that which we desire and then to begin to imagine scenes as if our desire were true. Stop 'wanting' and begin imagining as if your desire were true (releasing pounds, recording a hit song, meeting certain people, travelling to adventuresome places, etc.).

Start seeing in your imaging periods or sessions exactly what you want to see and feel as if it is real. See yourself receiving words of congratulations for accomplishing what you desire to do or be. See people shaking your hand or hugging you or sending you congratulatory letters or notes for what you accomplished. See yourself beaming from within at the joy of success. Feel everything as real as if it is already true, already been manifested.

Spiritual Exercise: Repeat to yourself while in bed falling asleep, "I am falling asleep in the assumption that I am totally healed, joyful, grateful, happy, relieved, blessed and at my perfect weight. I am in the state and assumption of weighing 150 lbs. I am deep in the state of not desiring to eat just food but what is best for me is my mind set."

Exercise: As you drift off to sleep, see yourself looking in the mirror and saying "My, (use your name here) I've never seen you look as beautiful as you look tonight. Your skin is glowing, your eyes are sparkling. Your smile is breathtaking." Subconscious mind will take it from there.

Nutribullet Blast- Do you want to feel good, eat healthy foods by adding cellular levels of foods, feel different about how you look and turn ordinary foods to super foods once a day? And have the best day ever? www.nutribullet.com for recipes.

    Suggestion: A Nutribullet Recipe that I use.
Nutribullet Blast- Turn ordinary foods to super foods once a day and have the best day ever.

> ½ cup washed spinach, kale or collard greens
> 1 stalk of celery cut in thirds or fourths
> 4-5 strawberries
> 4-5 peach slices
> Water to the MAX line
> Put extractor blade to work for 60 sec.
> Drink and say ummm this feels and tastes soooo good.

Brief Points of Chapter
- Using the same thought patterns, choosing to eat in the same way and the same foods which haven't worked for you is not benefitting you.
- We must train our imaging faculty, our *creative mind* and give it new instructions and new directions.
- Imagination precedes the desire fulfilled if the desire is not cancelled out by our disbelief. Start seeing in your imaging periods or sessions exactly what you want to see, feel as if it is real.
- Be specific in what you desire to be as a millionaire or to have millions for example, to be thin or to be slimmer, healthier and more flexible and mobile.
- Stop wanting and feeling you lack your desire, start appropriating it and begin claiming it.
- Feel yourself as that thing you desire. See it in your mind. Fall asleep with this mind and practice during midday in the state you desire to be.

Grow Thin While You Sleep!

Chapter 3
How to Recognize Your Stumbling Blocks

"I am melding myself into LIGHT. I feel so sleepy, very sleepy and full of health. I cannot be deceived. My thinness is in readiness and appears daily with new changes in store for me." Super Vita-Minds: How to Stop Saying I Hate You...To Yourself
~ *Daya Devi-Doolin*

Inner Conversations vs. God Talk

When you become more aware of your self-talk (ego wanderings) and how deprecating it can be, you begin to stop it and put your self-talk into reverse or change gears putting and allowing your God Talk to be in the driver's seat, so to speak.

You see better results if you make an arrangement with Creative Mind to take over, giving you other thoughts, other words to use and build yourself up. You'll be more aware of how you speak to others as well which make for better, harmonious relationships with family, friends, business associates, customers, clients, even strangers who might become your clients, etc.

To help you do this, here are 2 words or phrases that I recommend you eliminate from your vocabulary of self-talk as much as possible. Keep a journal daily and each time you catch yourself going there jot it down even if it's your fifteenth time. Make it a choice to eliminate the phrases "I can't" and "I don't know." "I can't" and "I don't know" are some of the most self-limiting words you can use. I can't lose weight; I can't stay away from chocolate cake, chocolate donuts, chocolate candy, and pizza. "I don't know", allows you to see yourself as not claiming your responsibility of knowing who you are. You don't respect yourself so how or why would anyone else respect you or your decisions.

My comment is that you do know, but you allow yourself to sabotage your God-Self (even though this can't be done). You do this to prove to yourself that you are weak and God is not there for you.

Henry Ford has a quote that says: "Whether you think you can or you think you can't, you're right."

You will experience your words in action when they mirror back to you through creative mind's manifestation of your reality to you and you'll wonder why "I can't seem to lose weight"; why "I can't seem to get a job with more pay than I'm receiving now". You will always manifest or it will always be manifested for you exactly what your thought has predominately been focused on. Your words, your thought, your vision and imagination create your reality.

When I told myself I was going to be able to re-learn how to play 4 chords this week on my guitar, my Creative Mind went about making that so, making me see a way to make the swelling go down in my hand and fingers as well as my arm. So my thinking made it so. And so it was!

You will manifest every single time what you think about and speak about. Creative Mind, Infinite Intelligence, Universe will render up situations to you in which you believe you can't or can do something and it will be so.

Take out the phrase "I don't know" from your vocabulary. It doesn't help you. It only hinders your progress and keeps you in the stuck mode. It's a stumbling block you must decide to get rid of quickly. It's easy. Just take your attention off "I don't know", jot it down in your daily journal each time you say it and it will become less and less of a burden or obstacle to your growth, your success in releasing the excess weight you have decided to release.

Try rephrasing the "I can't", into "I believe I can." "I don't know", into "I'll see if I can find the answer or do some research" or, "I'll see if someone else might be able to help me on it." "I'm going to give it over to my creative mind tonight before I drift off to sleep and I'll rest in the Peace of God." The answer will come to you if you allow and accept the package it comes in.

As I have said before, our thoughts, our words are our inherited gifts from God and they are very powerful. They create our external world and we want to use this gift wisely because we have to live in that world. Why not create a more perfect one, successful one, a happier one for ourselves?

As A.D. Luk's books, The Law of Life. Vol. I and II, explain, "The law of cause and effect is the law, the law of energy and vibration. The law is not someone's opinion, concept or theory but law, universal and cosmic, which is impersonal and that never did and cannot fail. The law works because of the feelings you put behind the word or thought and it releases currents from your I AM Presence which produces the manifestation."

If you say, "Well, I have spoken affirmations and denial statements and the law does not work." It has not worked because there has been some doubt in your consciousness and you put more faith and feeling in your doubt than you did in the desired end. Putting your faith in doubt enabled you to put other gods before you.

You are the law. You are the I AM Presence. You alone can call on your Presence to act for you, no one else can. A.D. Luk says, "The I AM Presence is the all-pervading principle in life, the most divine activity in the universe. It is the only active principle each one of us has. It is ever striving for expression to produce perfection through each of us.

I AM is the life principle in your body. It is the principle of life expressed through Jesus Christ. I AM is the creative word, the initial word that produced creation and from which all creation springs. The words I AM are the two cups that carry the power into outer activity. The use of the words I AM denotes individualized being."

When you invoke the words I AM, you are calling forth life into manifestation. It releases energy from your God source and it becomes manifest in your life.

If you are wondering as many of us have, why is my life this way or that and why can't I do anything about it to change it? The answer is you can, and only you can. You have made up certain erroneous laws about life and *your* life, which you are soon to discover if you do not know already. If you are ready, we can begin to discard those old laws, archaic tapes and replace them with Law of Mind.

I myself wanted to know what laws had I made that put me in the physical shape I was in (thought I was in, that of being overweight). When I was nineteen years old, I was five pounds overweight and decided that was too much. I had made up my law, which was unreasonable, so I had to become dissatisfied with myself because of my rule.

I wrote the laws down which attracted my overweight problem to me. I had claimed it as my 'problem'. They are listed below. See if they sound familiar for you.

These are the stumbling blocks I drew up as real.
- I don't listen to the Holy Spirit's guidance.
- I don't like my stomach or abdomen so I perpetuate my weight problem by not liking it (putting all my feeling energy into the hate and putting other gods before me); therefore my body had to keep itself in a state of that consciousness. Now I could continually prove to myself what I 'believe' was right, regardless of whether it was a lie.

- I believe food is 'fattening'. I believe I am guilty for eating and I believe I harm myself by the foods I eat. Rather than know all food comes from God and therefore no food is harmful to me except what fears I place upon it. I pretend to know what God is feeling while I live in my own ego consciousness world.
- I do not eat when I am hungry and I do not stop when the Holy Spirit tells me that I am full. I hear when I am full, but I ignore it and give myself excuses why I can't waste the food. I won't be good if I leave food on my plate. I do not realize that I can save it for a later day or even eat it only when I am hungry. The next process I had to undergo, in order to learn what laws I had made for myself that were not making me happy was to list the fears I had of letting go of the laws. What would I be losing if I gave up the problem?
- I have made myself believe that I am unworthy of good according to past relative's perception of me; so I had to prove to myself I was not worthy to live up to my expectations. I merely accepted those that were projected onto me. I did not know I could choose not to accept anyone's beliefs about me that were incorrect.
- Now I know I am worthy of all good. I Am the Good in all things. I Am Holy and every cell, nerve and fiber in me is Holy and knows it has the consciousness of Holiness.
- I am afraid I'll be a failure at releasing weight, therefore since I am afraid, that consciousness of fear keeps me in failure because of the energy I put into that false belief about myself. I always have to do what I believe even if it is false or negative because it proves me right. When I get out of the fear consciousness, by my choice, I'll know that nothing

can cause me to be afraid or overweight. I will know I am invulnerable, as a child of God, to any fearful thoughts.
- I keep saying to myself, "It's hopeless" instead of "It's hopeful." That consciousness of lack keeps me hopeless and fulfills my false image about myself. I am now full of hope. I AM HOPE!
- I trust my heart.
- I trust my heart.
- I trust my heart.
- I trust my heart.
- I trust my heart.

I felt the need to write these many times until I finally believed it and felt good about it. Perhaps you may find you will need to do this or something similar as Spirit leads you.

I also wrote:

- I, Daya, am now willing for my beauty to come forth and I am now willing for everyone to like me including people of my past, present and future.
- I, Daya the Christ, AM one with God. It is safe for me to be my ideal weight and be pregnant too.
- I, Daya, The Christ, can and do eat anything I want without feeling unhappy, guilty or shameful and no longer give my power to powerless foods.
- I, Daya, The Christ, love myself for eating whatever makes me happy no matter what it is. I choose to be happy about all things without being attached to it.
- I, Daya, choose to eat only when I am absolutely hungry and choose to stop before I am stuffed.

One of the things that was revealed to me by God is, "You are to forgive all your wrong thinking and give it all over to the Holy Spirit. Be at peace with yourself and know you are not alone. You are not as you think you are. Love dwells within you because you are Love created like Itself. Live in the now. Share loving, the gift I give to you. Give up your false beliefs, the ones you say you are in control."

I needed to know which steps to take to apply this to my life and so I was given some applications or blueprints for knowing, which are:

1. Know that I AM One with God.
2. Bring your bitterness to the Holy Spirit.
3. Forgive who you think you are.

"God's law is that I cannot be deceived." It comes from A Course in Miracles. I decided to find out what my laws were that tried to refute His Law in my life. What was it that puffed me up to be greater than He?

The Answer: My law is that I believe I AM overweight, so I am because I made up that law for myself. It manifested my truth for me to prove me right, to prove I am God punishing me. But I made myself unhappy by this truth just so I could be right. God's law is, I am my perfect ideal weight right now, underneath my illusion. Problem solved!

Some of my stumbling blocks were holding onto the consciousness that "I am fat. I am fat. I am fat." And so it was established for me as truth. To make my life happier, I had to embrace my passion and turn within. I had to reveal my negative emotions to my Higher Self and surrender that thought consciousness.

Doing that shifted my perception of fear and failure into success. I no longer wanted limiting beliefs that inhibited my success, my flow of life's energy. I forgave myself my mistakes, my error thinking about myself which removed those stumbling blocks of thought patterns that were not helpful to my growth.

I learned about EFT–Emotional Freedom Technique. It is an emotional version of acupuncture except needles are not used. It follows a 2 step process: 1. Mentally tuning into a specific problem & 2. Stimulating certain meridian points in the body by tapping them with your fingertips. It is an effective way of unblocking fears and limiting beliefs; plus, it is very portable and easy to learn.

What laws have you made up for yourself to believe in and prove yourself right, though mistaken and unhappy? Take a moment right now and write down in your journal the laws you have made up for yourself which may or may not be true. You can choose to change your laws, your thoughts about yourself and begin by knowing God's law is that "You cannot be deceived."

Spiritual Exercise: Repeat to yourself as you are drifting off to sleep, "I am melding myself into LIGHT. I feel so sleepy, very sleepy and full of health. I cannot be deceived. My teeth are solid white, strong, healthy and free of plaque. My gums are strong and pink. My thinness is in readiness and appears daily with new changes in store for me."

Check off which ones below apply to you and write them in the back of this book or your journal. Some of your laws could be:
- I am lonely.
- I am an alcoholic.
- I am alone, deserted and fearful.

What are your stumbling blocks of the past and what are your new God laws?

These were three of my other stumbling blocks and thinking: I used to drink tea with 3-4 tsp of organic sugar. I eventually said if I needed that much sugar, I need to quit, so I did no problem. Secondly, I also thought I had to add evaporated milk every time. Thirdly, I refused to listen to when to stop eating even though I was full. I learned to divide my food in half on my plate (restaurant or at home) and have it later if I wanted. If I felt I had to have a Dunkin' Donut, I'd buy one and put it in the freezer for a later time. Sometimes the later time was 3 weeks later. Then I knew I didn't 'need' it.

*Suggested Nutribullet Recipe that I use:
    Toxin Cleansing Blast
    1-2 handfuls of rinsed spinach
    1 cored pear
    1 cored apple
    1 cup of pineapple
    Water to Max. line
    *Nutribullet's warning is if you are taking any medication, please check with your doctor before consuming any of the Nutriblast recipes.

Brief Points of Chapter

- When you become more aware of your self-talk (ego wanderings) and how deprecating it can be, you begin to stop it. You put your self-talk into reverse or change gears, putting and allowing your higher self to be in the driver's seat.
- You will always manifest or it will always be manifested for you exactly what your thought has predominately been focused on. Your words, your thought, your vision and imagination create your reality.
- You will manifest every single time what you think about and speak about. Creative Mind will render up situations in response to what you believe you can or can't do and it will be so.

- The Law of Cause and Effect is the law, the Law of Energy and Vibration. The law is not someone's opinion, concept or theory but law, universal and cosmic. The same law applies to everyone. The law works because of the feelings you put behind the word or thought and it releases currents from your I AM Presence which produces the manifestation.
- I open myself to the greatest healing powers of the universe – that by the mere thought, I AM beautiful, I would be that. I deem sleep and rest are my options, and I would relieve myself from the burden of fear in order that my desire might be complete. My energy centers are opening and I am allowed complete and total rest in my being. I open myself to total and complete rest of the entire body as Golden Liquid Light comes through the top of my head through a divine invisible opening. It is Done!

Grow Thin While You Sleep!

Chapter 4
Feeling, Imagining, Believing

"If you want to find the secrets of the universe, think in terms of energy, frequency and vibration." ~Nikola Tesla

You Can Manifest Any State You Desire

Sound creates form. Whether the sound is inaudible or not or it creates form at some level. Thoughts are sound vibrations and they create form, become energy, vibration, a frequency and substance. When a thought is combined with strong feeling like belief, or conscious of a state desiring to be entered into or manifested, Creative Mind accepts this thought, this feeling as that of being the truth (whether erroneous or not). That thought becomes manifested into a form representative of the thought.

That thought vibration is picked up by your creative mind as that which you really and truly want objectified or manifested for yourself. It pleases us down to the minutest detail. Our conscious mind does not know how to deliver the reality of our thought form. Its job is to give direction and instruction to Creative Mind (Infinite Intelligence) and to let go and let God.

Our conscious mind sees things as we think they are not as they really are. Imagination is the truth of the state (consciousness) desired. Imagination creates our reality. It is what really creates our reality. That is our truly greatest gift besides having the Word (thought) as a part of our inheritance. As Neville Goddard says, the "Mouth of God is the Mind of Man". You can manifest any state you desire through imagination. You can image yourself healing someone 2,000 miles across the ocean. You can imagine yourself in your own business. You can image yourself with the best business or relationship ever possible for you when you see, feel and believe yourself in that situation.

You can see yourself slimmer, thinner and make that your reality when you place your faith, belief and acceptance of your imagination as that reality. See and feel, hear people congratulating you on your success at getting thinner, healthier and happier. Hear people congratulating you on how by your success, you have given other people help, motivation and inspiration to do what you have done with your weight, business or life for example.

From Mr. Twenty Twenty, "Believe you HAVE received. Not that you will, not that you might. Believe now that you have – received – that you are now the person you have chosen to be – that you have what you have previously hoped for." Mr. Twenty Twenty is the Founder of http://freeneville.com/free-neville-goddard-lesson-back-to-the-basics/

Spiritual Exercise: Give this command with feeling to your subconscious mind as you drift off to sleep. "I give you permission to boost my metabolism back to normal and please know I am deeply grateful and fulfilled." Feel it deeply when you repeat those words.

Suggested Recipe:
Energy Elixir
Add some serious pep to your step with this delicious and energizing elixir. A perfect afternoon pick me up.
2 handfuls of rinsed spring greens
1 banana
1 cup red grapes
1 cored pear

1/8 cup of walnuts
Water

Brief Points of Chapter

- It's very important for you (us) to BE that which you (we) desire to be and become BEING when you take your attention away from not being or not having. See yourself doing, having, being and living in the state of what you desire through your imagination, in your state akin to sleep.
- Make a game of the following short statements, sing these out loud, spin around and dance while you are alone, driving, waiting or whatever you may be doing. Enjoy and have fun while being whimsical!
  1. I inhale slimness.
  2. I exhale slimness.
  3. I love slimness.
  4. I Zumba slimness.
  5. I hike slimness
  6. I newscast slimness.
  7. I eat slimness.
  8. I dress slimness.
  9. I live slimness.
  10. I AM slimness.
  11. I play slimness.
  12. I dance slimness.
  13. I yoga slimness.
  14. I Pilates slimness.
  15. I do slimness.
  16. I think slimness.
  17. I act slimness.
  18. I BE slimness.
  19. I breathe slimness.
  20. I practice slimness.
  21. I skydive in slimness.

22. I write in slimness.

Grow Thin While You Sleep!

Chapter 5
Building a Consciousness of Thinness

"Faith is to believe what we do not see; and the reward of this faith is to see what we believe." ~Saint Augustine

See What We Believe

There is a metaphysical technique called "I remember when" that Neville Goddard taught. I have used it in my life. It's pretty simple and I was reminded of it when I entered into the Texas Longhorn restaurant today to meet friends. They were playing a song called, 'Remember When' and a male country singer was giving thanks for the memories he and he wife had loving, raising kids and seeing them go off to make their way.

I'll give a few of my examples of its use in a few moments. When you look at the present and are unhappy about what you 'think' you see as real then use this technique and you will begin building a thinness consciousness or a changed external experience will develop.

I picked up a piece of typing paper that was clean. I got a photo of my husband Chris all dressed in a tuxedo. He had been not too happy with the pounds he had put on. For about 25 of our 38 years of marriage he weighed about 175 lbs. He started to creep up to 190-195, 199 and was beginning to get concerned enough to change his eating habits. So in this technique, I wrote on the paper after I glued his photo, "I remember when Chris was not happy with his weight. Now he's back to being trim, healthy and slim, and a happy divine being."

So when you use this technique you change the future while in the present, in the now and you lift your spirit up and start to see there can be a new reality for yourself, physically, mentally and emotionally. You cannot be 'stuck' when you use your words in this manner.

For our finances on the same page, I glued $100 dollar bills (photocopy) in stacks of $10,000 packets. I wrote alongside the photocopy "I remember when we were poor, homeless, broke, and in debt. Now we're abundantly supplied and we know why we are wealthy and debt free. We've accepted our multiple income and allowed subconscious mind to work out the kinks and create the vibrational frequency necessary to match our changed view, changed perspective about our finances. We allowed God."

Early on in our marriage, we became homeless for seven months because someone in our band stole our rent money from our hiding place. By reading Catherine Ponder books for free in the Cambridge, MA metaphysical bookstore, we were able to see our first real income in late fall and move into an unfurnished apartment with no refrigerator. So, I could have written, "I remember when we were homeless, no income, no welfare, no car and no place to sleep out of the rain and cold weather. Now we have a beautiful home with a pool, pets and luxurious cars and multiple income sources."

When you use the 'I remember' technique, you are telling your subconscious mind things are better and better now and you are thankful. Subconscious mind acts on that truth and continues making things better and better for you. This technique takes you away from ungrateful to being grateful. It takes you from trying to figure out how to MAKE things better. You cannot do this. You do not know HOW. When you leave everything to the Christ mind – subconscious mind, imagination, you materialize far more than you could ever know existed for you to be manifested.

One of the other photos on that page was one of myself at a lesser weight in leotards, socks and sneakers outside of a motel room we had stayed at in Macon, GA. What I wrote was, "I remember when I was not grateful at my weight, but now I am grateful for my progress at releasing weight and eating better. I love you God. I love myself greatly. I love my faith in God and myself for I am a Divine Being."

Here again, you are impressing creative mind with what you know is the real truth even if you don't believe it right away and subconscious mind doesn't know if it's a truth or lie. It only acts on what you believe, what you feel to be true at the time. So why not give it happy thoughts and directions.

If you don't like your dad for how he treated you as a child, or hate your mother for being weak (an illusion just your perception) then when you use the 'I remember' technique, you could word it as, "I remember when I didn't like my parents for such and such, but now I do and I am fulfilled. I am grateful. I am happy." Clearing the limiting belief of fear of failure is a great place to begin your journey back to happiness.

Spiritual Experience: Inhale three deep inhalations and exhalations. Each exhalation, draw in the abdomen as far as you can letting go of all carbon dioxide, tension, stress and fears. On the next breath, inhale and hold the breath. Look into the quietness with your third eye (inner eye) all around and inside your body and mind. You will feel your rhythm spiraling. You will get in touch with your molecular rhythm, you will see and feel your molecules of light pulsating. You will be merging with your Self. Release the breath effortlessly when ready to inhale again. Repeat this process for as long as you feel the need, anytime of the day or night. If it's at night, just move on into your sleep for the night.

Suggested Nutribullet Recipe
1 handful of spinach
1 celery stalk cut into 3 or 4 pieces
1 scoop of Green super food (search online for Organifi or at the health food store for what you like)
Water to MAX line
AND

Plan a special treat for yourself. Decide to choose one of these for yourself for this week.
- Free yoga class
- Visit or sign up for a Zumba class

- Make a 2 gallon glass jar fruit infused water for yourself
- Spa treatment.
- Take a 20 minute walk.
- Take a nap.
- Give yourself a colonic treatment with certified Colonic Specialist.

Brief Points of Chapter
- When you look at the present and are unhappy about what you 'think' you see as real then use my techniques and you will begin building a thinness consciousness. As a result, a changed external experience will develop.
- When you use the 'I remember' technique, you are telling your subconscious mind that things are better and better now and you are thankful. Subconscious mind acts on that truth and continues making things better and better for you. This technique takes you away from the state of being ungrateful to the state of being grateful. It takes you from trying to figure out HOW to MAKE things better.

Grow Thin While You Sleep!

Chapter 6
How to Be Thin Right Now

"Stop thinking about the difficulty, whatever it is, and think about God instead. This is the complete rule, and if you only will do this, the trouble, whatever it is, will presently disappear."
~The Golden Key, Dr. Emmet Fox

Be Thin Right Now

When you decide you want fresh clean energy into your aura, into your mind, into your spirit, you must clear away the energy thought forms that aren't bringing the good you desire into your experience. You are what you think and there's no getting around it. "As a man thinketh, so is he." James Allen.

When you think lack, poverty, limitation, you believe it so strongly and so you prove it to yourself by giving that direction to your subconscious mind to supply proof back to you. When you think abundance, you are that abundance because you believe you are in the state of abundance.

Do you ever think about what you want to achieve in life and are suddenly overcome with self-doubt, panic and the feeling that you should just give up – before you've even started? Have you stopped yourself from even telling the people closest to you about your future plans because you JUST KNOW they have no faith in you or your projects? After all, they do say that life is beautiful but hard, don't they?

How do you handle big decisions when you are faced with situations for which you were unprepared? Do you admit DEFEAT before you even begin? Do you CONSTANTLY doubt yourself and put yourself down by thinking; "I can't do this, I might as well give up now"? Or do you go on with life carrying a firm conviction that in the end everything is going to be okay?

The most important trait in life is BELIEF in yourself, and in your abilities, belief in God's love. Is eliminating struggle and pain more important than magnetizing love, prosperity and calmness? I think so. Eliminating, releasing, surrendering the thought forms that created the struggling and pain in the first place, needs to be trashed, deleted, and recycled into the trash bin outside of your mind. When that happens, automatically, you will begin to attract the love, prosperity and joy into the empty spaces where fear was once lodged. It really takes as much energy to hold onto negativity as it does to think positively. Why not accept the better thought?

Live in knowing that the power of thought is our inherited natural gift and that God is always in Total Agreement with whatever thoughts we hold true and entertain as truth. Live in the NOW and experience everything around you to the fullest and with love. Allow yourself to Believe in the Law of Mind, the Law of Cause and Effect and know that consciousness is IT! It creates the world we see and we are the directors of this VAST creation as God is always in Agreement with all our creations! We can change the script at any time we are ready to move on. As you move through your day, know that The Holy Spirit is your Only Invited Guest! So that means anything unlike LIGHT cannot possibly enter your state of mind.

Spiritual Exercise: The technique below is one used by millions of people because it frees them to live the life they desire and to not be in bondage to their own beliefs of the past which have mis-created the present life they are experiencing now.

EFT – Emotional Freedom Technique. This process releases your fears and relieves blocked emotions and pain that have accumulated over the years within your body's cells, your emotional and spiritual cells. It is a psychological acupressure technique that helps your mind, body and spirit reprogram itself. You are giving instructions to your subconscious mind to draw unto you your desires. Some of the benefits are:
- Reduces Food Cravings
- Reduces or Eliminates Pain
- Implements Positive Goals
- Reduces or removes negative emotions

Before you begin, you must rate your feelings about being overweight, obese, heavy, or whatever term you wish to use about yourself even if it's about finances or career. You can go to the Internet and look up these names as a resource: Bill Yates, Dr. Joseph Mercola, Carol Look, Nick Ortner, Jessica Ortner and others including myself.
1. Rate your feelings about your fear concerning weight, finances, relationships, and your relationship with yourself, etc. from 0-10, ten being the worst feeling.
2. Repeat this following affirmation three times while doing Karate Chop (tapping with two fingers on fleshy side of your left or right hand), Even though I have this fear of _____, I deeply and completely, profoundly love, accept myself and forgive myself for having any fear (covers anger, resentment, bitterness, frustration, etc.). Repeat this statement that relates to only you 3x while you tap on the karate chop point. This is a very valuable technique. It will bring up your fear and you will release it.

3. Sequence: Tap between 5 & 10 times on side of either karate chop hand with two fingers as you repeat the above phrase.
4. Tap the top of the head (crown) (optional) repeat, Even though I have this issue (fear of being hurt, surgery, being weak, a victim, etc. or other problems, weight loss, I deeply and completely profoundly, accept, forgive and love myself).

TH	Top of Head
EB	Eyebrow
SE	Side of the Eye
UE	Under the Eye
UN	Under the Nose
CH	Chin
CB	Collarbone
UA	Under the Arm
WR	Wrists

5. Next tap the side eyebrow inside corner repeat, Even though I have this fear, I deeply and completely, profoundly, accept, love and forgive myself.
6. Next tap side of the eye and repeat the above statement. It won't do to have someone say it for you, but someone close and trusting can say the phrase and you repeat it after them. That would work.
7. Next tap under the eye and repeat above statement.
8. Next tap under the nose and repeat above statement.
9. Next tap chin, under lips and repeat above statement.
10. Next tap between the two collarbones (with two fingers) and repeat above statement.
11. Next tap under the armpit about three inches down and repeat above statement.
12. Take a deep breath or two. You should check in with your body and see if there is any remaining

discomfort or fear then you can rate it as 0-10. Repeat this process until a lot of relief is gained. You'll feel lighter in spirit.

- Even though you might still have some fear, realize that you could be happy to notice this so you can start accepting change in your life for the better.
- What is basically happening is you are communicating to the brain that a change is taking place and you want your body cells to receive this change of information and store the information in the heart center and other meridians. You won't be attracting what you don't want.
- Take a deep breath and let everything go. Where? Into God's Hand.

Do EFT about 10x a day for yourself or more. Whenever you stop for a moment, in a waiting room, office before lunch, in the bathroom, or any place and time you can do EFT.
America's Success Coach, Jack Canfield says, "You're unconsciously focusing on your fear all the time. It's your subconscious that needs to get reprogrammed. By focusing on it for a little bit of time (with EFT) we can get rid of it so it's not unconsciously running you."

Suggested Recipe:
This Life Boost Blast is a NutriBullet Recipe
Start your day with a blast of calcium and magnesium. No supplement ever tasted this good!

- 1-2 handful of rinsed kale
- 1 pitted peach
- 1 banana

- 1 handful of strawberries
- 1/8 cup flax seeds
- 1/8 cup of goji berries
- Water to the Max. line

Brief Points of Chapter
- You are what you think and there's no getting around it. "As a man thinketh, so is he." James Allen. This ties into the Law of Cause and Effect which is immutable in the universe.
- When you think abundance, you are that abundance because you believe you are in the state of abundance. When you think about thin-ness, you are that state of being slender because you believe you are in that state.
- The most important trait in life is BELIEF in yourself and in your abilities. The Holy Spirit is your Only Invited Guest.
- God is always in total agreement with whatever thoughts we hold true and entertain as truth.
- Allow yourself to Believe in the Law of Mind, the Law of Cause and Effect and know that consciousness is IT! It creates the world we see and we are the directors of this VAST creation as God is always in Agreement with all our creations!
- We can change the script at any time we are ready to move on.
- Use the EFT on yourself about 10x a day and practically anywhere, anytime.
- Take a deep breath, let everything go.
- America's Success Coach, Jack Canfield says, "You're unconsciously focusing on your fear all the time. It's your subconscious that needs to get reprogrammed. By focusing on it for a little bit of time (with EFT) we can

get rid of it so it's not unconsciously running you."

Grow Thin While You Sleep!

Chapter 7
Grow Thin While You Sleep!

"I will not hurt myself again today." ~ Lesson 330
A Course in Miracles

I Will Not Hurt Myself Again

Release fear-based thought patterns by surrendering what is no longer useful to you for your spiritual growth and that of our planet. Ask for angelic or Ascended Mastery help and guidance before you fall asleep. Allow your conscious mind to deliver your new blueprint, new images, and instructions on what you desire to change as you lie in bed. No worries, no anxieties, no doubts, only faith that it shall be so. Breathe in slowly, breathe out slowly.

Breathe in God and fill your lungs up fully and deeply. Breathe out disappointments which occurred during the day. Breathe in the Peace of God as you breathe out frustration you may have felt during the day.

You can re-write the day in your mind; thereby convincing and conveying to your subconscious mind a totally different picture for it to improve upon. This technique is called *Reversal*. You allow subconscious mind to magnetize continued reversed experiences and events to take place tomorrow as if it was NOW, in the present during the day for you. If you didn't get the results from a letter that suited you, then reverse the words in the letter to suit you.

Re-write the letter as you would have it read before going to sleep. Go back in your conscious mind and see everything reversed to the beginning of your day as to what you desired to see. There is a lot of power in doing this. Be grateful. Give thanks before falling to sleep for the wonderful day you had. The miraculous day you had will be impressed upon your subconscious mind and multiplied for you in the next present moment.

Allow the Universe to take over, surrender your ego's will to God, and release its hold on your long spent belief in illusions, of hatred of other races, of willful unforgiveness, of bitterness to other individuals such as your boss, that ex-husband or wife, to resentment of that relative that you think did you wrong in one situation or another. Then you will wrap your arms about God-Mind and return to a feeling of peace that you may have forgotten for eons.

Allow the Universe to take your pain, your illusions, your fears and hopelessness and create for you the influx of LIGHT into your entire body, mind and spirit that will change your course of direction. Let it happen for you! No work involved on your part – just to be open for the Good.

Sleep is another gift from God that allows you to be aligned most with your creative mind (subconscious mind) meaning your ego self is out of the way. There is no hindrance and it's also aligned with prayer. In the silence of sleep, you are allowing creative mind to do its work. In the silence of prayer you are giving permission for answers, solutions and guidance to be revealed to you. All you have to do is accept and act on the answers given.

This is what the Psalmist wrote for us and to understand it is shared by Dr. Joseph Murphy, "*Let the words of my mouth* (your thoughts, mental images, good) *and the meditations of my heart* (your feeling, nature, emotion) *be acceptable in thy sight, O Lord* (the law of your subconscious mind), *my strength and my redeemer* (the power and wisdom of your subconscious mind can redeem you from sickness, bondage, and misery)." Psalm 19:14.

Feed your subconscious mind the seeds of rest, health, relaxation, rejuvenation, abundance and prosperity in all you do as you drift off to sleep knowing that ALL is WELL.

Reversal Example:
You say to yourself: "At my center today, I taught a yoga class full of energetic, happy to learn students, happy to pay me my fee for teaching them. I weighed in at 145 lbs. today, having gotten a battery for my scale and released excess weight around my midriff. I saw 5 clients today new and old and each one paid me $100, two clients paid $500 for my wisdom and healing modalities used with them and my counseling. I gave more than what was expected. I sold packages of Young Living Essential Oil products and explained clearly how and what they could do to be helped by these essential oils and other products. I feel great and I am thankful."

Spiritual Exercise: Write down in your journal how your day can be reversed to the way you want to remember it. Your subconscious mind doesn't discern whether what you write or say is true or untrue. It just goes on the attraction mode and makes it into an effect of your imagination.

Suggested Recipe: NutriBullet
Free Radical Fighter
2 handfuls Swiss chard
1 avocado
1 cup watermelon
1 cup blackberries
1 fig
½ cup blueberries
1/8 cup flax seeds
Water to Max line

Brief Points of Chapter

- As you lay down ready to go to sleep, breathe in slowly, breathe out slowly. Breathe in God and fill your lungs up fully and deeply. Breathe out stress.
- Go back in your conscious mind and see everything reversed to the beginning of your day as to what you desired to see.
- Allow the Universe to take over and surrender your ego's will to God.
- Allow the Universe to take your pain, your illusions, your fears and hopelessness and create for you the influx of LIGHT into your entire body, mind and spirit that will change your course of direction.
- In the silence of sleep, you are allowing creative mind to do its work. In the silence of prayer you are giving permission for answers, solutions and guidance to be revealed to you.

Grow Thin While You Sleep!

Chapter 8
What Are You Willing to Change?

"Your subconscious will accept the stronger of two contradictory propositions. The effortless way is the better." ~Dr. Joseph Murphy

How to Meditate

Many, many people that I have met along my path have asked me out of the blue questions like, "How can you always be so peaceful? What do you do to remain so peaceful and calm? Can you teach me how to meditate?" Their questions take me by surprise and then I share with them what they are seeking to know. Chris always jokingly says things to me like, "Sweetie Pie, you need to learn not to be so stressful all the time", or "You're the only person I know on the planet who is not stressed out." Then we both get a good laugh out of it.

I learned to meditate or that there was even such a thing as meditation some fifty plus years ago from my gurus. I wasn't seeking to learn meditation because I had never heard of it. I was seeking to learn all about Yoga which I had heard inside and I wanted to know about it. It was a 'by product' as it occurred that comes along with learning traditional Yoga.

I wanted to change. I wanted a change. I may not have known what it was that I wanted to change but I knew I desired to change. I found out through that desire, that unwanted thought patterns were what was needed to be dropped in order for a new, powerful, energizing thought system to emerge and bring to me what I desired to see in my spiritual and emotional environment.

"Research from the National Center for Complementary and Alternative Medicine (NCCAM) also supports the notion that meditation acts as a form of 'mental exercise' that can help regulate your attention and emotions, while improving well-being. Even better, these changes may be permanent. It's been found previously that meditation prompts changes in the amygdala, a region of the brain associated with processing emotion. Newer research suggests these beneficial brain changes persist even after the meditation session is over, resulting in enduring changes in mental function." (http://1.usa.gov/15vvNy6), Dr. Joseph Mercola.

The Key to Meditating

The key to meditating is to realize you are listening to our God Source in the Silence and to focus on the breath. The mind has to follow your command and nothing else when you focus on the inhale and exhale. It cannot focus on doing two things at once.

Breathe in a seated comfortable position on the floor or chair. If you cannot manipulate sitting cross-legged, then a modified cross legged position works. Actually, you can meditate anywhere as long as you are not using heavy machinery or driving a car. You can meditate while doing the dishes or vacuuming the floor, taking a hike or sitting in your favorite chair.

Devote at least twenty minutes each time (work up to an hour) sitting before your altar, seated on your bed or on a chair. Practice any form of meditation or prayer that you are personally drawn to.

Sometimes what I do is light a candle, burn my favorite Incense, Nag Champa or another soothing scent. You can put music on that soothes and inspires you or use none. I don't always play music. Place meaningful objects on your altar, flowers and create a sacred circle around you with your intention. Call in your guides, angels, archangels or your spiritual teacher.

Being still, you focus on your breath, joy, stillness and being present. Feel your breath, or feel the blood pumping through you or focus on the candle light. Release random thoughts; watch them leave you by your command. Detach from them. Breathe.

You will notice when finished, a change in the way you feel, your energy will be light and you will feel different in the way you see things. Thank your guides and release them. I like to smooth my aura, swishing down and away as I know I am bringing loving energy my way. After meditation if it's at night, I drift off to sleep peacefully and release all cares, prayers to the Lord, (Law) to be demonstrated the next day to come. If it's in the morning, I practice my yoga asanas afterwards. I don't put myself in a rut by doing the same thing every day. I listen as to what I need to be doing and listening to my Guidance.

End your meditation by focusing the energy back into your body. I always thank my guides and angels. Notice how you feel after your meditation and feel how light but grounded you are.

Technique on Breathing, Relaxing and Healing Yourself

Why is this section important? It's important because if you do not breathe while you eat, dance, love, BE, you will not keep charged, energized, healthy or happy. Breathing as you eat, slows you down, you enjoy your food and notice when it is you get full and satisfied. Osho once said, "To be creative is to be in love with life."

Pranayama or breathing is for health, happiness and liberation. My yoga teacher, Prof. Yogi Bharat Gajjar is the first teacher I ever had who taught me Yoga, meditation and pranayama. His love captured me and has brought me to this point through fifty years as a teacher and continual student.

He taught our class the importance of the breath and how it is the Temple of our Health. You could tell he practiced and believed everything he taught us. His teacher was Swami Devananda and his teacher was H.H. Swami Sivananda. Swami Devananda had a great impact on Yogi Bharat.

I never knew breath was important. Nobody ever taught me about the breath or even considered the breath in my community of family, friends or church as being important. But I have since found out with Yogi Bharat and have since lived my life through my breath as it lives and breathes me.

Pranayama is yogic breathing and it's been practiced for thousands of years. Pranayama is using pranic energy that offers good health, more energy, and spiritual progress that removes toxins. Prana is the living force that is around everything and every human being. You can slow the heartbeat down and take in more oxygen in a shorter amount of time. You can also lower your blood pressure in minutes.

I teach several techniques in my yoga classes and one is called Kapalabhati, the skull breath. This cleanses and heals the body and brings a lot of energy into your brain and your skull. The human body uses the chest, lungs and abdomen. In yogic breathing, the diaphragm lowers to the abdomen as the lungs get filled with oxygen. The abdomen (stomach area), expands out or inflates. We're not concentrating on expanding the chest but expanding the abdomen so the lungs really get inflated and filled with plenty of oxygen.

Prana is not oxygen. It is an energy that circulates through our astral body and like I said, it's very healing. You can use prana during your meditation. It will bring you peace, quiet the mind and reduce stress.

There are yogic forms of sitting but for our case right now for beginners, just sit in comfortable chair. Eyes closed and sit straight. Keep your mouth closed and breathe through your nostrils.

Spiritual Exercise: Write down in your journal a list of things you want subconscious mind to begin working on for you. Do it quickly without too much thought or doubt about whether this can take place for you. If you know what you are willing to change, give infinite intelligence, subconscious mind permission to do it in a divine, harmonious way. Check your mood before going off to sleep. Sleep knowing you are wanted; sleep as you assume "I AM prosperous and I AM affluent. I AM a success." Feel as if you were in possession of your new weight-loss state of mind. Whatever you desire is God's desire for you. Quickly relax into feeling light. Feel as if your desire has been fulfilled.

Examples:

- What I desire tonight as I am drifting off to sleep is for my subconscious mind to arrange _____ _____lbs. to be released easily and effortlessly. I want to see and experience happiness around each cell of my body. I want my thyroid gland, (thymus, gallbladder, etc.) functioning easily and effortlessly.
- When you awake and after you do your meditation session, yoga session or peaceful ritual, write down what you want to see happen today. Imagine it as real.
- I desire to see family troubles dissolved, for example.
- All your books or articles sold.
- I desire to see peace for my children at school, peace on my job, peace with my clients or customers, peace in the marketplace.
- What do you desire today – to know more people, to have people pay for your services, to have thoughts change for the best, to see your weight in a different light, to have plenty of cash, money for a trip, breathing easily as you go to sleep tonight?

- Assume your desire is fulfilled and see the miracles take place.
- Share your experience with others so they can enjoy seeing things work for them as well.

Suggested Recipe: Hormone Balancer (female)
50% Boston head lettuce
50% mixture of fruit:
½ cup blueberries
½ pitted peach
1 tsp. Maca powder
3 Brazil nuts
Water to MAX line

Brief Points of Chapter
- The key to meditating is to realize you are listening to our God Source in the Silence and to focus on the breath.
- The mind has to follow your command and nothing else when you focus on the inhale and exhale. It cannot focus on doing two things at once.
- Breathing in a seated comfortable position on the floor or chair, if you cannot manipulate sitting cross-legged, then a modified cross legged position works.
- Devote at least twenty minutes each day (work up to an hour) sitting before your altar, seated on your bed or on a chair. This can be whatever space is sacred or peaceful for you.
- There is not ever too much you can ask creative mind to help you with.
- Prana is the living force that is around everything and every human being. You can slow the heartbeat down and take in more oxygen in a shorter amount of time.

You can even lower your blood pressure in a matter of minutes.

Grow Thin While You Sleep!

Chapter 9
Grow Thin While Helping Others to Reach Their Goals

> *"Forgive yourself and everyone else before you go to sleep, and healing will take place much more rapidly. Guidance is given you while you are asleep, sometimes in a dream."*
> ~ Dr. Joseph Murphy

Grow Thin While Helping Others

There is no one person more special than another. Each one of us has a gift or gifts to share with the world, our fellow brothers and sisters. Each one can learn from someone else and help someone. As you live your life being led by a higher power, you will shed light onto someone else's life without even knowing that you had such a positive effect on him or her.

Give your full attention to someone who is speaking to you. Share your compassion when someone calls on you but keep yourself distant from their drama, so you won't get pulled into their energy field of fear or anxiety. You can be of better service when you do. Show them how they can rise above their fears and doubt and give them what you know to be Truth when they ask for it.

Be open, honest and truthful about everything to yourself and others. Remember thoughts are things. Your thoughts are powerful, energized thought forms that can bypass time and space. Thought is one of our most powerful inherited gifts from the universe. It is our Word made flesh (manifest) from the invisible ethers into the physical. Thought with intention, belief, desire and faith makes the invisible known in the visible, without doubt.

Once you know that thought is the cause which has an effect, you will not have thoughts that you think are idle or neutral. This is because you will find out that there are no neutral thoughts. You find out that there is nothing to fear and that nothing unreal exists. This will shine through from you when you are with others and will quietly bless them and quietly inspire them.

Ego's use of guilt, anger, blame, judgment or criticism keeps us in a prison. What we give out we receive while in that prison. You can change that thought pattern now. By doing so, you are then helping others to conquer and to become their own Master of their situation.

Changing our perception of what we see shows us the miracles that are before us. We could ask that the true meaning of what we see or experience be revealed to us. Instead of seeing ourselves as limited (ego's view of ourselves) and lacking, unhealthy, getting old, weary, unloved, or being overweight, we could turn those thoughts over and begin to see ourselves as totally whole, safe and secure. Make the changed thought pattern be the one you feel strongly about like, "I believe I am getting slimmer, more trim, healthier, and even younger looking."

Give creative mind permission to help you see a trimmer you. Ask creative mind to show you, for example, the ways to increase your stamina while exercising; or create the type of menu you need to switch over to; or get you a mentor who is an expert on releasing weight; or a weight training expert near your home. Don't put limits or think that creative mind doesn't know what to do. Put your faith in your guide, who is an expert at delivering to you exactly what you have asked for by putting your feeling, imagination and your desire behind it.

The vibration of these words alone, such as "I am whole, safe and secure," "I am trim and happy at my results," will make it so. Stating with belief and conviction, "I am my perfect weight," will make it so. Saying, "I have more than enough money to have fun, travel and serve others," will heal your lack of prosperity image immediately. The Light from these words focuses energy into the dark cells of our being and radiates love everywhere, within and without. It allows us to walk on water so to speak, (overcome any turmoil in your life).

The next extremely important thing in life is to be totally grateful for everything you see around you, in your inner and outer life. That is how we change things, by being thankful, not by being critical or judgmental of yourself or anyone.

The first step is to be grateful for the space in your consciousness that you have graduated to. Next, you can move into an even more limitless consciousness and become more of a servant to mankind on the level of unconditional love. Being grateful transmutes all negative energy blocks in the cellular, emotional/mental and spiritual level throughout the entire body.

When you see ego in its rightful place, which is that of a sunbeam instead of our Creator, you will automatically get off the treadmill of statements like, "I hate myself, I hate my body, my hair, my buttocks, my teeth, I hate my life or I hate the world." Instead, you can now say, "Thank you, ego, for letting me know that this is not the path I want to be on. Thank you for showing me there must be better consciousness to be in than what I have mis-created. I am grateful that I can change. I am grateful I am Master of my Life! I am grateful creative mind has shown me a better way."

We all have power behind our intentions and thoughts. I have explained how thoughts are things and how to use them to our advantage. I have shown you the importance of changing our perception about ourselves in order to see the miracles that are waiting before us in a parallel reality. I have given some examples for applying the principles and techniques for you.

It has been my intention to show that you can become empowered enough to know that you can change your life, relationships or any illness, simply by the positive way you feel about yourself; also, by believing that you can do so. Put yourself in a 'feel it real' state of mind so you can hear in your mind people congratulating you on how you pulled yourself through. See them telling you how beautifully young you look, how much happier you are and what a changed attitude you have taken on. Before you know it, you will experience the desire that you have been longing for, for a long time.

Anyone can come to realize that she is a beautiful and loving being. We deserve all the love that is meant for us to have. We can give our goals the power to manifest boldly and securely in our lives by having faith in things unseen, faith in a Higher Power and the energy that we put behind our faith. What is there that is difficult to manifest in our lives? Nothing, if we but believe that it is possible.

Make it your personal intention to give yourself permission to sit in the seat of receptivity of your highest good. Part of that intention could include having a fantastic healthy looking body, feeling great, or a beautiful career that uplifts thousands. You can intend to keep sustaining and nurturing the love of yourself and developing deep abiding friendships. You can intend to write the necessary diary entries, articles, newsletters and even books that create new avenues to explore for yourself what you are guided to experience and share with others.

Believe that you can make your life a blessing for all that come in contact with you. Make your intention a powerful one and it shall be done unto you. We are taught, our word will not come back unto us void. Make your intention to Love Yourself as powerfully as you can make it. Do everything you can possibly do to have fun while doing this. Let your joy BE in the doing for yourself and celebrating yourself. Bless yourself every single day and give thanks always for the beauty within you. Know that your love is with everyone as you begin to look past illusions from the 'outside in'.

When we totally and completely love our "Self", there is absolute trust and faith in all our decisions, because we are recognizing the Self that we truly are. Your Self can make no mistakes, because we are operating from Love and Love cannot be anything unlike itself.

Uplift those you see who are willing to ask for your help, to be strong in spirit and to know that ALL IS WELL. Remind them they must be willing to align with that Spirit that has things in store for us greater than anything we can imagine.

There are many universal tools we have been given to use. I have learned to incorporate them in my life and in my family's life in order that we live a healthy, happy lifestyle. You are given the same opportunity to use these tools and techniques. You will see the *Door of Everything* open itself to you leading the way to the many mansions beyond it that are there for you to experience.

Spiritual Exercise: Repeat this tonight as you are lying in your bed, "I AM prosperous in thought, creativeness and happiness. I am supplied by the Universe far beyond my fondest and wildest dreams. Joy flows through every part of me as I lie here. I draw unto me all the people I need in my life in the most wondrous ways." Never go to sleep unhappy, dissatisfied, disgruntled, or angry at yourself or others. Decide to release it and let it go. It's for your good.

Suggested Nutribullet Recipe
½ cup chopped pineapple
¼ cup blueberries
½ cup papaya
Several strawberries
Water to the max line

Brief Points of Chapter
- What are you willing to change or stop doing that is not serving you?
- What can you do for yourself today that is very loving and kind?
- What can you say to yourself today that you have never said before that proves you are worthwhile and deserving of your love?
- What would you like someone to say to you to show that they appreciate you for what you do for them? Ask them to tell you. Feel how that feels.
- Sitting in the seat of receptivity – what do you want creative mind to put on the platter that is waiting for you right now?
- What can you say or do that will uplift someone?

Grow Thin While You Sleep!

Chapter 10
You Are Thin Right Now!

"This is my holy instant of release." ~ Lesson 227
~ *A Course in Miracles*

Your New You

Sitting in your seat of receptivity, breathe deeply about 3-4 deep breaths through your nostrils. Allow the Lotus Petals on the crown of your head to open up for you in your crown chakra, God's love and Light. Allow yourself to finally be at rest, to be at peace, to be in the zero point zone where we hear all we need to hear in the Silence. You are Thin right NOW! This is your reality beyond your illusion you have about yourself.

Your seat of receptivity is anywhere you choose to sit and you are quiet, sitting in the stillness with your breath, your intention of receptivity from Spirit. Open your consciousness to that of being one with the Universe, knowing the Universe is within you and you are in the Universe. So you wait and accept and act once you have received.

Do you feel that YOU are worth the gift that the Universe has laid out for you? My hope for you is that you make the transformation, so that you are not going to find yourself in an unyielding prison of mind. Tell yourself this gift is what you've been waiting for and you are bathing in its holy presence.

Before falling off to sleep, have your head equal to your body, flat with no pillow. Count up to 50 and repeat with feeling, knowing you are instructing Creative Mind

(Infinite Mind), "I am falling asleep in the assumption I am totally healed, joyful, grateful, happy, relieved and blessed to be thin again in mind and body."

1. I always think of images for the state (awareness or consciousness) of my desire.
2. I am in the state and assumption of weighing ___ lbs. and I am deep in the state of eating just the food that is best in my mind for me guided by Creative Mind.
3. For business then, a possible statement for you to use could be, "I will sit here or fall asleep imaging that I am seeing clients paying me handsomely without guilt on my part for receiving my excellent care, loyalty, integrity and support for their well-being."
4. I get up excited every day for my increased strength, courage, changed belief patterns, new blueprint that my Creative Mind has given me. I can do this. I have done this. I am thin, right NOW! I don't have to force myself to believe this. It is my gift to know this because my thoughts have been reprogrammed and acted on by Creative Mind.
5. I have surrendered my ego's way of doing things which were not working for me. It did bring me to this point in my life where I know it is not my Father as I had believed and so I am grateful for this.
6. "Be not afraid. There is nothing to fear." A Course in Miracles.

Here are some tips for you before I say goodnight to you until the next chapter. These tips come from Mr. Twenty Twenty, Founder of www.FreeNeville.com regarding Neville Goddard's teaching. "Your job is to simply PRUNE your vine – keep training your imagination to come FROM the state of the wish having been fulfilled instead of letting it 'think about' that state.

1. The true vine (and what creates your circumstance) is your own wonderful human imagination. When you believe this you will no longer imagine as you formerly did, but will prune your thoughts every minute of every day. You will break the habit of feeling remorseful, depressed, or regretful. You will no longer think unkindly about another, because you will know that he is actually yourself pushed out, and appeared in your world because the Father in you called him.
2. The difference between 'thinking about' and 'feeling from' is subtle at first. Thinking about the state creates anxiety, and often has bits of 'when' you want it to happen (implying that it 'has not' and bits of 'how' you want it to happen) which is the TINY ego trying to take over Spirit's job. Feeling from the state – I know that I am that woman/man – and I create and react to the world – from that state.
3. When you imagine, it is God in action. He is the true vine and the vinedresser, for he is your imagination, imagining you. If you really understand this, you will start pruning your thoughts. If you don't and continue to believe Jesus Christ is other than your Self, you will persist in allowing your wanton energy to run wild, to swell into irregular twigs, and bear unlovely things in your world." *~Neville Goddard*

Brief Points of Chapter
- Your seat of receptivity is anywhere you choose to sit and you are quiet, sitting in the stillness with your breath, your intention of receptivity from Spirit.
- Before falling off to sleep, have your head equal to your body, flat with no pillow. Count up to 50 and repeat with feeling knowing you are instructing Creative Mind (Infinite Mind), "I am falling asleep in the assumption I am totally healed, joyful, grateful, happy, relieved and blessed to be thin again in mind and body."
- I get up excited every day for my increased strength, courage, changed belief patterns, new blueprint that my Creative Mind has given me.
- The true vine (and what creates your circumstance) is your own wonderful human imagination.
- When you imagine, it is God in action.

Grow Thin While You Sleep!

Summary

I have learned what ego is and that it is nothing but fear. It is simply a thought system we have mis-created. We have allowed it to separate ourselves from the Prime Creator (the thought of separation itself is an illusion). It keeps us a prisoner or slave to habits and personal thought patterns. It keeps us stuck in day-to-day life situations until we say, "Enough! I surrender all illusions about myself to the Holy Spirit." Ego blocks us from accepting our good because we do not feel we deserve our good or deserve to be loved.

I am the Christ just as Jesus Christ is and so are you. I know and believe we are endowed with the Christ Consciousness just as He is endowed with it. Jesus is perfect. He always chose to listen to the Holy Spirit. He never allowed idols like anxiety, fear, jealousy, condemnation, judgment and fear of lack of money, distrust or dissatisfaction, to be His 'Father.'

We choose these idols to be our 'father' and then allow ourselves to be dissatisfied with the manifestation that these choices bring about. These choices keep us in a vicious cycle by choice.

Jesus was the Master of His physical life because He chose to think high vibratory thoughts that radiated in and without His being. He did it to show us that we too can be the Master of our lives. He did it to let us know we do not have to crucify ourselves every day with condemning thoughts about ourselves. It is a choice we make, to listen to the voice for ego or the Voice for God, the Holy Spirit.

It has been my personal intention to sit in the seat of receptivity for my highest good. Part of that intention includes having beautiful holy children, a beautiful luxurious, holy place to live, a flourishing metaphysical healing center and services that touch the lives of others, a fantastic recording career that uplifts thousands and positive uplifting metaphysical books that heal with His Word.

I intend to keep sustaining and nurturing the love of myself and developing deep abiding friendships. I intend to write the necessary books, articles and newsletters that I am guided to write. I intend to reach millions of people who are seeking and desiring to change their lives for the better.

My philosophy includes believing that you can make your life a blessing for all who come in contact with you as well. Make your intention a powerful one. Make your intention to Love Yourself as powerfully as you can make it. Do everything you can possibly do to have fun while doing this. Let your joy BE in the doing for yourself and celebrating yourself. Bless yourself every single day and give thanks always for the beauty within you. My love is with everyone and I hope you will begin to look past illusions from the 'outside in' so you can know your love as well.

When you totally and completely love yourself, there is absolute trust and faith in all your decisions, because you are recognizing the God-Self that you truly are. Your God Self can make no mistakes because you are operating from Love and Love cannot be but loving.

A quote from Marianne Williamson is, "The universe is intentional. It is always moving in the direction of greater love, regardless of whether or not we consciously align with that love.

When we do align with it, we thrive. And when we do not, we suffer. This is not 'punishment'. It is merely the Law of Cause and Effect. With each thought we think, we either align with universal love, or we disconnect ourselves from it. Whichever is our choice determines whether we then feel connected to, or disconnected, from our own true Selves."

I have led you to know and experience some of the many Universal principles and tools you can use at any time and I have incorporated them in my life and in my family's so that we experience living a healthy mental and spiritual lifestyle.

We see the *Door of Everything* open itself to us and we walk through the many mansions beyond it that are there for us to explore. You can do the same thing with your pure Intention.

Grow Thin While You Sleep

Appendix

Your Workbook for 7 Days

This is your workbook for 7 days. You can choose to repeat the full 7 day task for a total of 21 days. This will help instill new habits for your body, mind and spirit.

Day 1 Consciousness is IT! It creates the world we see and we are the directors of this VAST creation as God is always in Agreement with all our creations! We can change the script at any time we are ready to move on. As you move through your day, know The Holy Spirit is your Only Invited Guest and that is something I encourage you to really realize, remember and utilize for any of your desires!

Subconscious mind is another name used for creative mind. Other names for the same force are Infinite Intelligence, Infinite Mind, and God-Mind. Repeat to yourself aloud whenever any kind of temptation arises "The Holy Spirit is my Only Invited Guest Now!" Repeat it every 4 hours minimum. Write down the results or the changes you have noticed within yourself just today.

Prepare a Nutribullet blast for healthy muscular system

Blue Builder
50% spinach
½ avocado

1 cup blueberries
12 almonds
1 tbsp. flax seeds
Water or almond milk to top with water or almond milk to MAX line

Day 2 Ego's use of guilt, anger, blame, judgment or criticism keeps us in a prison and what we give out we receive while in that prison. What else does it do? It lives in fear, acts out of fear and blossoms into illusions glorified.

Giving is having and giving is receiving. If we give out judgmental thoughts, critical thought, words or deeds, it is exactly what we are proclaiming to manifest in our lives. Changing our perception of what we see shows us the miracles that are before us.

Notice what miracles you have seen today. What have you given today that you have never given before to yourself or anyone else? Write everything down. How did you feel? What or whom did you criticize if at all? Was the Holy Spirit Your constant Guest today? How could you tell? What took place that you can describe into words?

a.

b.

c.

d.

Prepare a Nutribullet blast for Anti-aging:
Berry Buddy
50% Kale
½ avocado
½ cup blueberries
½ cup blackberries

½ cup raspberries
Water or almond milk to MAX line

Day 3 We can decide now and that's what I am assuming you are doing now, deciding to change your blueprint or pattern of thinking to one where you realize, that everything you think does matter if you wish to change your external world to one of success instead of failure. We have a conscious mind which is concerned with seeing life as we think it appears. It sees death, sickness, poverty and limitation, etc. of every kind and it impresses the subconscious mind with its belief that what we see is true and is the truth. The subconscious, is simply power, without direction. It does what it is directed to do with no judgment by the faith and belief we have invested in. Whatever man feels deeply or images clearly, is impressed upon the subconscious mind, and carried out in the minutest detail.

- What illusions did your conscious mind make you believe was true about yourself today, about your weight? Did you invite the Holy Spirit as your only guest when it happened? What was the next direction you took after that happened?
- What does subconscious mind do for you easily and effortlessly? What are you willing to give it permission to do for you tonight as you drift off to sleep?
- What is the role of the subconscious mind?

Day 4 When a thought is combined with a strong feeling like belief, or conscious of a state desiring to be entered into or manifested, Creative Mind accepts this thought, this feeling as that of being the truth (whether erroneous or not) and that thought becomes manifested into a form representative of the thought.
1. Is this true or false?
2. Is Creative Mind the same as subconscious mind?

Prepare a Nutribullet recipe for a beauty blast. One that I have used:
Cider Cup
50% Swiss chard
1 cup red grapes
½ one raw beet
1 Brazil nut
1 tablespoon (Bragg's my favorite) apple cider vinegar
Water to Max line

Day 5 Read this aloud to yourself 2x today, which is from Sarah Young's book, *Jesus Calling*, "I, THE CREATOR OF THE UNIVERSE, am with you and for you. What more could you need? When you feel some lack, it is because you are not connecting with Me at a deep level. I offer abundant Life; your part is to trust Me, refusing to worry about anything.

It is not so much adverse events that make you anxious as it is your thoughts about those events. Your mind engages in efforts to take control of a situation, to bring about a result of your desire. Your thoughts close in on the problem like ravenous wolves. Determined to make things go your way, you forget that I am in charge of your life. The only remedy is to switch your focus from the problem to My Presence. Stop all your striving, and watch to see what I will do. I am the Lord!"

What is your experience after this spiritual exercise?

Prepare a Nutribullet blast for Better Night's Sleep:
Sleepy Seeds
50% spinach
1 banana
¼ cup Raspberries

¼ cup Blueberries
1 tbsp. pumpkin seeds
1 tbsp. sunflower seeds
Water to Max line

Day 6 What is God's Will? What is God's Will for me today? Is God's Will for me to worry about anything this moment? Is it God's Will that I lack any good thing? Is it God's Will that I be in need for anything? The answer is no to these questions.

Repeat these statements to yourself and align with the vibrational energy of them, feel them and believe them because they are true for you.

- God's Will for me is to be happy and free from thoughts that bind me into or with fear.
- God's Will for me is to look into my mirror and see how beautifully I was made from a seed into an embryo, into a fetus and into a baby in the womb.
- God's Will for me today is to find there is a smile worth a million dollars within me.
- God's Will for me is to walk, take a bike ride, take a yoga class, learn Pilates, learn Zumba, take dance lessons, go hiking, play tennis, racket ball, etc.
- God's Will blesses me and all my organs, glands, tissues, muscles, skeletal system, my circulatory system, my respiratory system, my joints, my brain, my entire body, mind and spirit.
- It is God's Will that my skin is clear all over. It is God's Will that my thyroid gland and thymus are back to normal and working free of hindrances.
- God's Will is that my heart, pancreas, liver and gallbladder are all functioning normally now.
- God's Will for me is that I am now free of All addictions to food, drugs, smoking, lusting, jealousy, coveting, being greedy, loathsome, lazy, procrastinating, etc.

- God's Will is that I am affluent, beautiful, giving, happy and free of hatred and un-forgiveness and live in a beautiful dwelling.
- God's Will blesses me, my family, my business, my job, my career, my home, my creative ideas, my finances, etc. My thoughts do not bless me when I am dwelling in 'lack' consciousness about anything. My thoughts bless me when I realize and know I am God's Will. I AM that I AM.

What are my spiritual blessings and experiences after Day 6? What did I come up with as God's Will for me?

Write your experiences below.

Prepare a Nutribullet blast for a healthy skeletal system. One that I have used; collard greens, turnip greens, mustard greens, spinach and kale are great sources of both calcium and vitamin K. I sometimes change from the water to organic apple juice, organic lemonade, orange juice, almond milk unsweetened:

Berry Bone Builder
50% kale
1 banana
½ cup raspberries
½ cup blueberries
¼ cup wheat bran
10 cashews
2 tbsp. raw cacao
Water to Max line

Day 7 By resting this day means,

- I give myself permission to allow God's Will to be listened to, adhered to and to give thanks that I hear God's Will for me.
- I give myself permission to allow God's Will to solve what I perceive to be 'my problem.'
- I give myself permission to allow God's Will to be done.
- I give myself permission to believe God's Will is for my good to be established.
- I REST now.
- Drink plenty of water each day!!!

Grow Thin While You Sleep

About the Author

Daya Devi-Doolin has been in touch with the Christ Consciousness since about 10 or 11 yrs. years old. She grew up in a broken family – but father was always nearby, touchable, loveable and very giving. She has a sister who lives in Philadelphia and another sister who lives in Houston, TX. She has a brother in Pakistan and one brother who passed away. Her mother raised her children up in the Baptist church and every Sunday, it was Sunday school and the children were all baptized.

When Daya Devi-Doolin was 35 years old, she had a profound vision. The vision showed a picture of Christ where his heart was revealed to her and she was shown that HE was branded into her chest over her physical heart. She wept when she saw this and felt the power of His Presence knowing He was branded within her.

She has had many such experiences with things of this sort during her entire lifetime. Those experiences led her to the path of Yoga with the Sivananda Yoga Center for 50 plus years of practice and studying. She eventually became affiliated and Registered with Yoga Alliance and has been in good standing with that international association for 12 years.

Daya Devi-Doolin is an Ordained Minister, and an Ordained Priest of the Melchizedek Order. She is the CEO of The Doolin Healing Sanctuary. She is an internationally known award-winning author and professional motivational speaker on metaphysical and self-growth books and topics. She is also the Co-Founder of The Doolin Healing Sanctuary with her husband Chris Doolin. Her inspirational speeches share her secrets for a successful life through our empowering thought system.

She has assisted thousands of clients over the past 25 years. She is the best-selling author of, The Only Way Out Is In: The Secrets of the 14 Realms to Love, Happiness and

Success!; Super Vita-Minds: How To Stop Saying I Hate You....To Yourself and a NABE Pinnacle Book Achievement Award Recipient for her books, The Only Way Out Is In: The Secrets of the 14 Realms to Love, Happiness and Success! and another NABE Pinnacle Book Achievement Award for co-authoring Americans Saving Ourselves Together: How to Thrive in the 21st Century.

She received an EDC Creations Literary Award for The Only Way Out Is In: The Secrets of the 14 Realms to Love, Happiness and Success! book in the Non-Fiction/Motivational Category. She writes inspirational songs along with her husband, performs and plays guitar under the Duo name of aka Level Seven with her husband Chris. Their music is distributed and sold by Amazon, Barnes and Noble, Padaran Publications. ReverbNation Company. They are members of BMI.

Her philosophy is "Thoughts are things. Thoughts are energy, substance and form. They draw unto themselves the likeness of their kind. We have the power by our Word to form all that we wish to create or mis-create." ~Daya Devi-Doolin

To learn more about Daya Devi-Doolin, go to:
www.padaran.com;www.akalevelseven.com
http://www.facebook.com/DayaDeviDoolin
Twitter: http://www.twitter.com/DayaDeviDoolin

Meet Daya Devi-Doolin in person at book lectures and signings, workshops, of Grow Thin While You Sleep Webinars/Seminars or Yoga Retreats. This is a great way to make your success more real. Meditations on her forthcoming CD will be available soon.

The Anointed & Appointed Ones

The following friends I call 'The Anointed & Appointed Ones' because they were the main ones who were instrumental in assisting in my physical, mental, emotional and spiritual recovery, besides my husband Chris and two sons, Tyler and Joseph. They went beyond the call of duty to respond to my rapid healing and I thank them here.

Inez Bracy

Inez Bracy, Lifestyle Transitions Coach, Speaker, Award-Winning Author, Radio and TV Personality helps boomer women rejuvenate, reinvent and redefine their life. Having used the science and art of reinvention, rejuvenation and redefining herself many times, Inez started her coaching business in 2005 to help boomer women deal with the sometimes overwhelming prospect of starting a new life in their boomer years.

Through the medium of TV, radio, teleconferences, training seminars and workshops, she has helped tens of thousands deliberately create a life by design. Inez draws on her personal experiences, training and excellence to share with audiences those essential elements that comprise her vision of leadership, vision, retirement success, fun, life, and faith.

As an accomplished CEO, a brilliant coach, and a gifted communicator, Inez brings enormous innate enthusiasm, insight, and energy to her presentations. As the creator of SPICE (Sassy-Phenomenal-Inspired-Conscious-

Empowered), Inez believes that each woman has the right to unleash her femininity and live the life of joy she desires.

Inez has been featured on Lifetime TV, The Balancing Act, giving tips on how to start your own home based business. She is a frequent guest on the Fox 4 Morning Blend as their Career Coach giving tips to help boomers successfully navigate the workplace. She is a columnist for the Coastal Breeze Newspaper, Senior Stuff, and former columnist for The Island Voice.

Inez Bracy
Inez Bracy International, LLC President
Lifestyle Transitions Coach, Speaker, Award-Winning Author,
Radio and TV Personality
(386) 748-5484
Inez@InezBracygmail

Debbie Moran

Debbie Moran is a Certified BodyTalk Practitioner, a Parama BodyTalk Practitioner and a Licensed Massage Therapist, Reiki Master Teacher and Certified NIA Instructor. She trained directly with Dr. John Veltheim and has been a BodyTalk Practitioner since 1998. Debbie has been a Licensed Massage Therapist since February 1992 and maintained a successful private practice in Tampa Florida until 2004. In 2004 she moved to Sarasota Florida and established a successful practice in The BodyTalk Clinic of Sarasota right next door to the IBA Headquarters.

In addition to her personal practice she has a substantial Distance Practice working with individuals, families and animals. She specializes in Parama BodyTalk and has taken all advanced courses including Animal BodyTalk, introductory PlantTalk, Mindscape, Manual Lymphatic Drainage, Holographic Cascading, Breakthrough I and II, FreeFall, Advanced FreeFall, Body Chemistry, Traditional Chinese Medicine, Parama and Parama Philosophy as well as Parama College Courses.

Her massage training includes certification in BodyTalk, Breakthrough, Manual Lymphatic Drainage, Reiki, Shiatsu, Touch for Health, Cranio-Structural Integration, Reflexology, Swedish, Sports Massage, SET and Deep Tissue Mobilization. Debbie is also a Certified NIA Instructor.

Debbie used to consider herself a student of Life and now considers herself to be a lover of Life. She has studied numerous philosophies and Spiritual traditions, some of which include Sacred Geometry, Matrix Energetics, A Course in Miracles, Mysticism, and Silva Mind Control & Ho'oponopono. She is dedicated to personally embody what she teaches and sharing those teachings in her day to day life. She is interested in helping individuals realize their own well-being and awaken to their own inner truth and Self-empowerment.

Debbie is available for individual appointments, for Distance Sessions, for Public or Group Lectures or to teach Modules I and II of the BodyTalk System, Advanced Practical Weekends and BodyTalk Access. She also teaches Nia classes to anyone interested in learning healing through movement and body awareness. You may reach her by phone at (941) 923-9300, by email at debbie.moran.lol@gmail.com or by writing to her at the following address.

BodyTalk & Beyond
2376 Fruitville Road,
Sarasota, Florida 34237.
Office 941-444-7479
Cell (941)-923-9300
debbie.moran.lol@gmail.com

Dan Towey

Dan Towey is another friend who drove to our home from Orlando several times to do cranial therapy and massage work on me. He is a LMT and entered the Massage Profession in 1992 after already being in the Wellness Industry for four years. After graduation from the Florida School of Massage with 1,100+ hours, Dan began exploring options with several certifications including Sports and Injury Recovery. He became involved with the FSMTA and realized a dream of becoming a 1996 USA Olympic LMT while also co-coordinating the Central FL chapter's Sports Massage Team. He's also honored to have mentored hundreds for the last two decades. Dan has been employed part-time with several chiropractors, three prestigious spas, sports race management and chair massage companies while building a client base. Being an active and highly competitive age-group triathlete for 18 years gifted Dan with several injuries (never once requiring surgery) which in turn had direct application for his clients.

Dan Towey, LMT, CRT, BF

www.DanTowey.BrandYourself.com
dantowey@earthlink.net
Access Bars Facilitator
Cellular Hydration Specialist and Independent Enagic Distributor, Inc
Hydration and Wellness Expert Educator
(407) 447-7294   Orlando, FL

Drs. Phil & Nalani Valentine

http://www.lulu.com/content/2166333

Drs. Phil & Nalani Valentine played another vital part in my healing as well. They both provided spiritual healing and naturopathic medicine for my smooth healing. Dr. Phil is Hygienic Scientist; Naturopath; Metaphysician; Clinical Hypnotherapist; Polymath, Lecturer; Free-Thinker. He is the founder, director and pastor of the Temple of the Healing Spirit; Self-Healing Education Center, The Institute for Self-Mastery; and The University of Kemetian Sciences. He is a certified member of the International Association of Counselors and Therapists (I.A.C.T.) and he received his Doctorate in Hygienic Health Science and Classical Naturopathy from The Life Science Institute of Texas, now merged to the Fit for Life Sciences Institute-College of Natural Health in Canada. A former member of the American Natural Hygienic Society, Dr. Phil Valentine is currently a Hygienic Science and Metaphysical Health Consultant to doctors and lay practitioners as far away as

Azania (South Africa), Canada, Trinidad, Jamaica, England, Ghana, Japan and the Philippines.

His wife, Dr. Nalani is the 'Home Life' Educator of the Deltona Women's Association, a chapter of the National Women's Association whose sole function is raising money for deserving charities. A nutritionist for over 40 years, Dr. Nalani is currently a Wellness Educator for NSA Juice Plus+.

In 1977, Dr. Nalani began a 30 year language career as an Interpreter and teacher of American Sign Language (ASL), which eventually took a secondary position to her career as a Holistic Practitioner.

In 1996, Dr. Nalani was diagnosed with breast cancer. She met and saw Dr. Phil Valentine as a Naturopathic Healer and he helped her to heal herself, using the same principles that are in her book, "7 Steps to Healing and Wellness, Using Essential Oils and the Kybalion as a Guide", without the use of pharmaceutical medication, and she has been cancer-free ever since.

Dr. Nalani enjoys helping people see the connection between what we eat and the quality of our health; in her sincere, people-friendly manner, she takes the mystery out of the healing process, while empowering her clients to take control of their own lives.

Nalani Valentine, ND, PhD, (known as Dr. Nalani) is a Naturopathic Doctor of the Hygienic Sciences. She is the founder of New York's Heal by Touch Wellness Oasis, and Co-founder of The University of Kemetian Sciences Online.

Photo by Maurice Starr

Chris and Daya Devi-Doolin
Aka Level Seven CD's available
www.akalevelseven.com

Email: Padaran@padaran.com

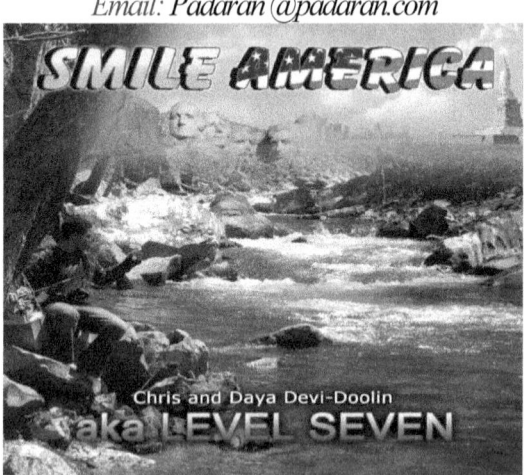

Rev. Daya Devi-Doolin is available for individual appointments for Reiki Training & Healing (Distance Healing using Usui Reiki), is an Ordained Minister available for Spiritual Counseling, Hatha Yoga Training, Public and Group Lectures on self-growth, Law of Attraction, Prosperity, Motivation, Yoga and related metaphysical and spiritual topics. Daya is a 'Dr. of Thought', and has studied numerous philosophies and spiritual traditions, some of which include Matrix Energetics, Reconnective Healing, A Course in Miracles, Ho'oponopono and EFT. You may reach her by email at Padaran@padaran.com. Her website is www.padaran.com for books and other products or services and www.akalevelseven.com for CDs and books.

She is a featured TV/Radio Guest, Speaker, Healer, Contributor and Writer for various blogs and websites such as:
www.VividLife.me;
www.examiner.com/x-35011-Orlando-Yoga-Examiner;
www.selfgrowth.com/dayadevidoolin
www.Facebook.com/dayadevidoolin
www.Twitter.com/dayadevidoolin.
www.blogtalkradio.com/padaran.

Rev. Daya Devi-Doolin
The Doolin Healing Sanctuary
Email: Padaran@padaran.com
www.padaran.com

Resources:
www.Nutribullet.com
www.eft.com
www.TAT.com

Journal Pages

Journal Pages

Journal Pages

自序

生在困难时,长在动乱期。少儿时期,因为粮票和布票的限制,虽不敢说吃不饱、穿不暖,但也尝到过饥饿的滋味,经历衣不遮体的窘样。不仅少衣缺粮,而且没有书读,偶尔得到几本"黄书",便如饥似渴、囫囵吞枣式地开始消化书中的内容,于是对中国的历史、文化和诗词产生了极大的兴趣。

老邓的东山再起,使得我们这一代有了上大学的机会。在大学期间,除了专业课外,有了机会和条件阅读到更多的文学和历史书籍,同时开始琢磨起了平平仄仄,后来因多次的迁徙,那些表达和融进了青少年的青涩和对未来的期盼的许多"诗词"丢失殆尽。

中国的诗词历史悠久,若从《诗经》的起源算起,诗词的历史恐怕要比中国的文字历史更久远一些,因为人们普遍认为,先有诗后才有文字。遗憾的是,这种起源于民间的优美文学、文化、历史的载体,逐渐地被演化为文人们摇头晃脑、显示才华的专用体材,更有后来的"钦定"诗韵和律规出现,使得律诗成了千篇一律、毫无生气的东西。

同时，这种"御用"和"八股"化，使得大多数中国人对诗词感到"望尘莫及"，更谈不上欣赏和继承。

语言的发展和声韵的变迁，使得所谓的"平水韵"或"钦定"诗韵已经不能适应诗词的发展和当代人们的文学创作，所以我们在创作律诗和诗词时，应当以中国现代语音标准为基础的《新韵》为依据，应运普通话四声和平仄区分的原则。当然，新韵不否定历史遗留下来的各种韵律规则。近几年来，笔者先后创作了几百首用于表达思想感情和人生感悟的诗词，在这里选了一些比较好的，将它们收集成册，留为纪念。

国泰无缘成勇武，只凭诗酒养疏慵。

唐规宋律文八股，取舍传承不盲从。

作者愿与所有的诗词爱好者和广大的读者一起，为继承和发扬中华民族这一宝贵文化遗产作出贡献。

www.ingramcontent.com/pod-product-compliance
Lightning Source LLC
LaVergne TN
LVHW051846080426
835512LV00018B/3103